LemonAid CHRONICLES

Stories of Pitfalls, Passion, and Purpose that Result in Payday!

- Tearanie Parker
- Jacqueline Andrade
- Kimberley Davidson
- Kimberly Jenkins
- Patrice Robbins
- Davida Bratton

LemonAid Chronicles ~ Stories of Pitfalls, Passion, and Purpose that Result in Payday! Copyright © 2015 by Jacqueline Andrade, Davida Bratton, Kimberley Davidson, Kimberly Jenkins, Tearanie Parker, Patrice Robbins

All rights reserved. This book or any portion thereof may not be reproduced or used in any manner whatsoever without the express written permission of the publisher except for the use of brief quotations in a book review.

Printed in the United States of America

LAC Publishing

ISBN: ISBN-10: 0692479805
ISBN-13: 978-0-692-47980-3

Unless otherwise indicated, all Scripture quotations are taken from the *Holy Bible, New Living Translation, copyright* © 1996, 2004. Used by permission of Tyndale House Publishers, Inc., Carol Stream, Illinois 60188. All rights reserved.

Scripture quotations from The Authorized (King James) Version. Rights in the Authorized Version in the United Kingdom are vested in the Crown. Reproduced by permission of the Crown's patentee, Cambridge University press.

Ordering Information: Quantity sales. Special discounts are available on quantity purchases by corporations, associations, and others. For details, contact Kimberly Jenkins at the information below.

Info@IamKimberlyJ.com
(757) 574-0704

Special Thanks to Shyla Miles

Edited by: Joylynn M. Ross, www.enjoywrites.com and
 Mary McBeth, www.UrbanFictionEditor.com
Book Cover Designed by: Nfuxion, www.nfuxion.com
Graphic Illustrations by: Fashionlistcally Speaking, www.fashionlisticallyspeaking.com
Layout and Interior designed by: www.interiorbookdesigns.com

Acknowledgements

The realism and the power of this chapter is a testimony to God for His amazing ability to turn what almost destroyed me into something good. You have truly taught me a lot regarding divine purpose. I love you Father, more than words can say. My deepest appreciation to my handsome husband, James Lopez Parker, you have always challenged me to be extraordinary. We have been through a lot together, but we are still here! You are an incredible father to our children and an amazing supportive husband to me. Words cannot express how grateful I am to the Lord for giving me you. To my four remarkable children, Bria, Stephanie, James Kyle, and Aiyana, each of you are a special treasure. You have taught me a lot about unconditional love and perseverance, may you understand deeply the concept of financial blessings through obedience and prayer and always walk under an open window. Lastly, I am grateful to my mother, Tressie Osborne, who was the first person to pour spiritual wisdom into my life. Thank you for being a great example of demonstrating the power of prayer.
    ~Tearanie Parker

I am grateful to God for never giving up on me, for believing in me when the weight of the world felt like it was crushing the very life out of me. I realize now that the weight was God's hand on my life pressing out the weakness in me, and removing the doubt and fear. God is faithful even when I am not. Thank you God for this amazing life you have given me and the awesome people you allow to bless me every day. To my family, I love you more than words can express; you inspire me to do better, for this I am thankful. I love you!

~Jacqueline Andrade

I would like to first thank my Lord and Savior Jesus Christ for being my EVERYTHING and for loving me unconditionally no matter what. Thank you Lord for the precious gift of the Holy Spirit who leads and guides me and for making everything I am and everything I have possible. I would like to thank my children, Khalil, Aasia, and Chaz for giving me the strength and courage to do more and to be better. Mommy loves you so very much!! I would like to thank Ms. Veronica McMillan for being like a mother to me when I needed it the most, for truly caring about me, and for your heart and motivation and standing in the fight with me. To Kim Jenkins, a woman who also has an amazing heart and spirit, thank you for all that you've done for me. To my girl, Aziza Ireland who I've known since High School and who I've been rolling with since then, thank you for always being there for me anytime I needed you whether to listen or encourage with absolutely no judgments. I want you all to know that I love and appreciate you all to pieces!

~Kimberley Davidson

As with many writers, I'd be remiss not to thank God for my trials and tribulations that have made me the strong, God fearing, self-confident woman I am today. I thank Him for blessing me with parents, Elvas and Iona Boyd, who raised me to love God, respect my elders and respect myself. I'm so grateful for the foundation and encouragement I've received and continue to receive from them still to this day. My fine, sharp as a tack husband, Dr. Harry Jenkins, my friend, "road dog", and soul mate (yes, he deserves that intro)--Thank you for loving me unconditionally and teaching me to trust again. Just as importantly, you love my children as your own—ain't God great! My best achievement and greatest show of love from God—my 3 beautiful and awesome children, Kaitlin, Brendan and Chandler whom I love to life--Thank you for giving me "my why" even at my lowest and my "amen" when I sit back and see the wonderful, loving people you have turned out to be. I can't forget my friends and family who have always had my back. I love you all!!!

~*Kimberly Jenkins*

I thank my Heavenly Father for seeing me through this difficult journey. Even when I was scared about the outcome, I knew you were with me and would give me the strength that I needed to make it through. While my medical team played an important role in getting me better, I am aware that my healing comes from you. "... for I am the LORD that healeth thee "(Exodus 15:26). I would also like to thank my parents for sacrificing their time and lives to take care of me. Your uncon- ditional love and support made getting through this journey much easier. I'm blessed to have parents like you. Thank you to my amazing brother. Even though we are miles apart, your love and words of encouragement motivated me to fight even harder. I would like to thank my friends for all your prayers, cards, texts and phone calls. You all will forever have a special place in my heart. Lastly, I would like to thank Vida Bratton for including me in this project. You continue to inspire me to

pursue the purpose God has for me. Thank you for providing me with an opportunity to share my story.
~Patrice Robbins

Thank you GOD!!!!!! Really! It has been nothing but your Holy Spirit that has helped me stay this course. Thank you my husband, Tyrone Bratton, who always believes in me and never gives up on me. You constantly encourage me that I can do it. I love you! Thank you Micah and Matthew for loving mommy through this process. You have kept me grounded by reminding me what really matters. And to my mother who has been my #1Fan since the beginning, you have seeded into me that I can do and be anything with God as my source. You were correct. And to the amazing authors on this project who rode this train for just about a year; you ROCK!!! This project would still be in the lulls if it were not for one particular team member, Kim D. We all love you girl!
~Davida Bratton

Table of Contents

Preface 1
Introduction 3
Chapter 1: Funding an Empire 5
Chapter 2: God, What About Me 19
Chapter 3: The Woman Behind the Hat 35
Chapter 4: A Polished Woman 61
Chapter 5: The Fight of My Life 87
Chapter 6: Bankrupt to Breakthrough 101
The LemonAid Process (Workbook) 117
Biographies 141
Afterword 157
LemonAid Journal 159

Dear Sister,

My prayer is that *LemonAid Chronicles* will bless you. This book was written to inspire all women beyond their current circumstances and know that a Payday awaits them.

It is my hope that you do not get discouraged in your current situation. The six of us have all been through some things and can attest that it is only temporary and you must hang in there! You will come through whatever it is equipped with the ability to help someone else.

LemonAid Chronicles are real life situations that have happened to everyday women who are educators, mothers, wives, business women, and women who love and have a relationship with the Lord. It has taken a little over a year to write this book and boy has it been a journey! It seems like as soon as we made up in our minds to do this, life just started to happen all around us. Some of us were out of work, juggling multiple jobs at one time, trying to figure out what to do next, yet still finding time to go before the Lord and press.

We have learned and want you to be encouraged that all things work together for good to them that love God, to them who are the called according to his purpose (Romans 8:28, KJV). Your change is coming.

With All His Love,
Vida Bratton

Introduction

Hi, Ladies! I am Vida Bratton, and because you have picked up this book, you are in for a ride. This project was birthed from a group of women coming together based on a desire to spring forward. We galvanized under the pseudonym *Team Take Possession* and decided to connect regularly. I conducted success trainings on relationship building, business, ministry, and entrepreneurship utilizing social media, and we began to soar.

As a result of the energy created via *Team Take Possession*, I asked the women if they would be interested in writing a chapter about their experience, which was mostly regarding social media, my area of expertise. But then something happened. A shift occurred. We began to discuss all of life's episodes that led us to even wanting to live life on purpose and launch our dreams. One conversation led to another and we found ourselves writing about the story that occurred in our life that shifted everything.

One morning while half asleep, I began to ask God to reveal to me the subject of the book and give me a subtitle that would ignite a fire in those who would read it. And I tell you He did just that! It was like nothing I had ever experienced. It summed up the essence of the book and the question many Virtuous Womenprenuers have: *How does all this mess result in anything? Thus, How Pitfalls, Passion, and Purpose Result in Payday!* It was given to me in an instant. I rolled over to my husband and told him. His immediate reply was, "Yes! That's it!"

This book is for the woman who is all too familiar with the surface ebb and flow of life and is ready to move into purpose. It is for that woman who needs an extra push, encouragement, motivation, inspiration, and application that will serve as a springboard from pitfall to payday. That woman who knows there is more to life than her current situation; the woman who can't figure out why life is looking hopeless sometimes with seemingly no light at the end of the tunnel. There is light, though, Virtuous Womanpreneur. There is a payday ahead!

This book was written because graveyards are full of purpose while pitfalls squelched desire, visions, and dreams of too many. We decided, NO MORE! We are forerunners for you. We hold the lamp and light the way. We do not claim to have all the answers, but we are connected and fully rely on the One who holds the future in His hand. We know that life comes with lemons. And we are here to help you make delicious *LemonAid*. Welcome to *The LemonAid Chronicles: How Pitfalls, Passion, and Purpose Result in Payday!*

Chapter 1

Funding an Empire:
God, Why Can't You Just Write Me a Check

Tearanie Parker

> God is in the sadness and the laughter, in the bitter and the sweet. There is a divine purpose behind everything and therefore a divine presence in everything – Neale Donald Walsch

Question

Would God give you a dream, open doors and then suddenly allow the doors to close in your face?

~1~

Twenty million dollars. That's the exact amount I wrote on the check to myself before tucking it away in my closet. Ever since I heard of a celebrity doing this as motivation for success, I thought, *Why not do the same thing?*

From the beginning, I wanted to be a teacher. I came from a family full of educators, and also pastors, and teachers of the Word of God, so walking in those same footsteps was an easy task for me. However, as soon as I became a teacher, I quickly decided that I wanted more. My desire was to own a chain of Christian schools from Pre-K to fifth grade. The idea was to give children a strong foundation in not only education, but also biblical principles as well. Sounds perfect, right?

I was extremely excited, motivated, full of joy and anticipation on how great my life was going to be. God was with me, so there was no reason I would not succeed. My faith was at an all-time high because I believed I was walking in my purpose, and for the most part, I was right on track. Doors were opening up without hesitation. I was so close to the finish line, I could taste it. It was simple; I was going to change the world with my "God-given" vision.

During the process, I found this large, three-level home located in a quaint area in Norfolk, Virginia. Everything about the place was perfect—location, size and price. At just a glance, my mind had already mapped out the floor plan of my entire school. To get the ball rolling, all I had to do was go before the Civic League and ask for the zoning to be changed. Piece of cake…or so I thought.

I attended the Civic League meeting, which consisted of a few nearby residents and the owner of the home I wanted to purchase. I gave my presentation as requested, by and large, everyone seemed on board; everyone except one woman. I thought nothing of it. Besides, the majority ruled that my idea to open a school in their neighborhood was a good idea. As a result, I was invited back for another meeting. I didn't know it at the time, but this had been the ultimate setup.

When I went back to present to the Civic League again, the *entire* neighborhood was present. I'm talking about cats, dogs, fish, squirrels from the trees—okay, I'm exaggerating, but the place was really packed! Apparently, the reason for this expansive turnout was an email that was sent out to everyone regarding my "little" vision. The same people who were once agreeing with me were now showing their true colors.

Where I had presented before in front of a few people, there were now approximately 70 or more. The entire plan had been centered on stopping me. I was somewhat disturbed at first, and I could see the odds were against me. However, I didn't expect that they would unanimously vote the school down. *"No, we do not want this school here."* I was frustrated, angry, but nonetheless, determined. I was convinced that God had told me to do this. Not getting it done wasn't an option. Like many times before, I prayed, fasted, and sowed financial seeds. Now that I'd recuperated from the severe blow, I began preparing for the next step.

I was informed my only remaining option was to go before the City Council. Just like before, when I presented to the Civic League, I was well aware that the odds were, once again, against me. But this time, deep down inside, I knew I was going to lose. Twenty-four hours before the big day, that inkling became stronger. However, something greater inside me said, "Go and still fight." For some reason, I had to go through the battle.

The next day, I firmly stood before the City Council, chest out, head high. I watched and listened as men and women from the neighborhood got up and spoke against my dream…my purpose. Person after person, I saw it being torn apart right before my eyes. Rightfully angry and full of hurt, I anticipated the final vote from the City Council. My request to start a small Christian school was denied. For the first time, all hope died inside of me.

I asked, "Where are You, God?"

"Why didn't You help me?"

"Why would You open the door and then close it?"

I'd pulled out all the equity in my home because of this "so-called" dream! I'd already been approved for the money to turn the home into a school. Why was He not helping me? I couldn't grasp why God would let me down like this. Wasn't this my purpose? There had to be a reason, a good one. But what was it?

God will open another door... The thought strongly entered my mind. What I hadn't considered was that the door I was trying to walk through may not have been the one intended for me. Was it really meant for me to open a Christian school? Nonetheless, I ignored those thoughts and kept pushing anyway.

While on my hunt to find another building for my school, I met two owners of a well-established Christian school who were looking to sell. The wheels began churning in my head. With the parents, teachers, children, and curriculum already in place, the hardest part was already done. This HAD to be God. He had given me a better, readymade facility, and soon enough my vision would be manifested. Once again, I could not have been more wrong.

The owners of the school wanted me to immediately buy the building *and* the business. Where it had once been an easy victory to get my hands on the appropriate funds for a school, I was now running into all kinds of roadblocks. In a nutshell, out of five banks, not one was willing to loan me the necessary funds. *Back to square one*, I thought. I went for what I believed would sway things back in my favor; I prayed, fasted, and sowed financial seeds. The idea here was, "God, if I continue to pray, fast, and sow into Your kingdom, You will help me fulfill my purpose."

Continuously, I asked Him to send me all the resources needed to make this dream happen. "Lord, why can't You just write me a check? Please God, fund this empire that I am building for you." As wonderful as it sounded, it never happened. God did not write me a check, nor did He send someone with the money to help me. While I was still trying to come up with the funds, the owners decided not to sell after all.

Devastated beyond words, I ended up taking a job as a preschool teacher at a Christian school. I felt like I had failed, but most importantly I felt like a failure to my husband and my children. I mean, every ounce of hope I'd ever possessed was gone. To go from almost owning a school—telling all your friends and family—to back to where you started, was soul crushing. Broken was putting it lightly. Tears, tears, and more tears…my dream was dead.

However, something inside of me kept wondering what went wrong. At what point did I get off track? I had many unanswered questions and the only one who could answer them was Jesus. Even though I was undeniably angry, I could not get angry with God. I needed Him. However, I did not hide how I felt. I told Him how upset, disappointed, confused, and hurt I was. I knew He would never leave me, but yet I felt all alone. I just couldn't understand it.

Sometimes, when I would get in His presence, I had no words. All I could do was cry. It was during those times that He began to do something great inside of me. My spiritual eyes began to open, and suddenly I began to see things clearly from His perspective. This dream of mine, had it really been of God or had it been of me?

For three years, I prayed and sought Him like I never had before. One day while in the bathroom praying, I cried out words that would change my life. "God, I give up. Whatever You want me to do, I'll do. What is your purpose for me? Before the foundation of the world, what did You have in mind when You created me? Tell me, Lord. I'm listening."

Have you ever heard the phrase, "Be careful what you pray for?" Well, let me tell you, God heard me, and He answered! From that point on, my life started turning in another direction. I began to realize that just because God opens a door, does not mean He won't close it. He is Sovereign. Sometimes God WILL allow you to go through things to mature you for His purpose, His dream.

Through various situations, good and bad, God began to show me that He wanted me to go into the financial industry. Huh? Talk about a drastic change of plans…I was not totally convinced. In fact, I was far from it. Before, I was so gung-ho about my so-called dream, this time I counted the cost. I waited on God and assured the timing was right. Most importantly, I made certain this dream was indeed from God.

I was so hesitant to move forward without God, that I asked Him to give me all kinds of confirmation, and He did. Five different people came to me (the same number of banks that had turned me down in the past) to tell me that I needed to be licensed in the financial industry, or some would say a licensed professional in the financial industry. The next step for me was to pass the Securities

Licenses Exams—the difficult, dreaded ones that I'd heard horror stories about.

During the process, all I could think of was how in the world is *this* line of work for me? I'm in debt and I need to be more knowledgeable and equipped to help people. Well, lo and behold, I became a Financial Advisor. This was the beginning of another new journey. However, the BIG difference was that this is what God had for me and not what I had chosen for myself. So, while it didn't happen overnight, it did come to pass. God was faithful.

After being in the financial industry for a short while, God began to speak to me about my own financial situation. When God calls you to be a catalyst for change, regarding the financial destiny of others, He begins with you first. The challenge for me to get out of debt was resonating in me greatly. I also began to look deeper into my commitment to tithe, and doing so on a consistent (not convenient) basis. The greatest challenge, however, was preparing financially for the generations to come. In other words, saving, investing, and managing money wisely. I began to clearly understand why I was placed in the financial industry. With the financial knowledge that I was acquiring, individuals and their families, my children, as well as my grandchildren's financial destiny could now change for the better.

My entire perspective about money changed. Having come from a single parent household with three siblings, I was not taught about money, the importance of having a good credit score, or how to make wise decisions and stay out of debt. My mother did the best she could, but my ignorance regarding finance led me down a path of bad financial mistakes. Little did I know, that my own experience would help me help others. Most people I meet have similar situations or mindsets that I'd once been accustomed to. I became a vessel that encouraged change in that I could relate and help them see their financial situation in a better light. This is something I could have never imagined in a thousand years. But that's how God works. His purpose for our lives is rarely ever what we think for ourselves, His timing, His way.

The funniest part about life is how much we think we know, how in control we think we are. I wanted that Christian school so badly that I was willing to dismiss my true calling. However, the signs were always there along the way. There was a reason I did not receive a loan from any of those banks. There was a reason those people fought to keep my school from happening in their neighborhood. There was a reason the doors opened and then closed. It was deeper than anything seen on the surface. I am still a teacher, I'm just teaching people in a different arena.

God didn't write me a check and it wasn't in His plan to do so. I was already living beyond my means spiritually, emotionally, and, of course, financially. I needed to be changed, mind and soul. In my ability to accept my purpose, financial strongholds that have even the richest of people trapped mentally, were released from me. I thank God for His wisdom and the contagious effect it has had in my life. I thank Him for allowing me to learn and share that being rich or poor has little to do with money. How you utilize the resources God provides and keeping Him first determines the legacy you will leave. Even if you don't receive all the money you are asking Him for (like twenty million dollars), just know that whatever He gives you will be all you'll need to not only fund your empire, but also equip others to fund theirs.

~ Many are the plans in a person's heart, but it is the LORD's purpose that prevails. **Proverbs 19:21(NIV)**

Chapter 2

God, What About Me:

My Journey to Finding Purpose

Jacqueline Andrade

> "You will never walk on water if you don't get out the boat."

Question

Ever been mad at God?

~2~

Ever sat down, looked at your life and thought, *God, what about me?* You don't mean to question Him, but all natural explanations just aren't making sense. Everyone around you seems to have everything they've ever dreamed of: a wonderful family, enormous house, and a flourishing bank account. You're not jealous…rather confounded.

I wasn't always on the outside looking in. At one point, I, too, "had it all." A loving husband, frequent traveling, great finances—basically, I felt the Lord had blessed me with abundance early on in life. Being saved was like adding the icing to my pretty good lifestyle. Since I stayed prayed up, I figured getting whatever I wanted came with the territory of being a faithful Christian. Ask and you shall receive. In my immature state I treated God as if He was my personal vending machine. I insert a prayer, out pops the blessing. Easy-peasy!

Well, six years into my "happy marriage," my husband came to me with the *we- need- to- talk* statement. We all know that is never good in a marriage, right? He told me the most humbling words I'd ever heard: "I don't love you anymore and I don't want to be married. I'm done."

Ouch! I may have been "okay" with that in any other situation. However, we had two very young children, had just sold one house to have another built, and were stuffed in a tiny one bedroom apartment during the interim. To add to the stress, in order to pay for this new bigger house, I would have to go back to work fulltime. Ugh! And if all that wasn't enough, my husband was moved from first shift on his job to third shift. This meant he would be working overnight from ten in the evening to six in the morning. I felt railroaded, attacked and confused by this overwhelming season in my life. What does a good God-fearing, Master's-Degree-in-Christian-counseling, mother of two, say to her husband who utters those words?

"We didn't marry for love. We made a commitment. Love has nothing to do with it. We stood in front of our family, friends and God, and made a commitment that will be honored. There will be no walking away. Do whatever you need to, regroup and get it together, because my kids need and deserve a fulltime father. I took vows with a fulltime committed husband. And just for the record, I don't love you either, and right now—I don't even like you. I know we are going through a rough patch, but we are not each other's enemy." That's what she says!

My husband's face looked like he thought I was crazy. He returned home the next morning, and praise God, we worked it through. But make no mistake, it wasn't easy. For the first time I questioned where God was in my life. I felt abandoned. I still saw glimpses of Him, but never like it had been during the better spiritual years of my life.

Financially, I didn't have much room for complaining. My husband and I were both employed by the state of New Jersey. Because of his job, overtime was always in demand. He filled that demand whenever possible, which alone landed us in a higher tax bracket. In addition to working fulltime for the state, I went into the cleaning business with a "friend," as well as a medical supply company.

Money was coming in from four different sources, in addition to my husband's overtime income. We were doing pretty well. The money I needed was at my fingertips. I was working like crazy and so was my husband. However, I was starting to feel greedy. That year we took the first ever Nickelodeon Cruise, which included us renting a private yacht in Jamaica for five hours. What a fabulous vacation! I smile from ear to ear thinking of all the fun we had and all the money we spent. Yikes! I felt untouchable. Then again, this is what we had worked so hard for. We ate at expensive restaurants three to four times a week, spending, on average, $200 each sitting. Of course, nothing stays the same forever. I hate change.

While reading a book, I came across a memorable quote. "You'll never walk on water unless you get out of the boat." Well, my boat—my comfort zone–was all of this "stuff" around me. It was the things I could buy with my earnings. Giving up completely wasn't something I'd been willing to do. Even so, the Holy Spirit directed me to leave my job. Thinking I could outsmart God, I eased into it by resigning from my employment with the state of New Jersey. I wasn't uncomfortable yet, because I still had two more businesses on the side, both to which were making great money. Three months in the economy started going downhill. Slowly, my businesses did too.

Since people were no longer vacationing, all the cleaning contracts I had with rental properties at the shore were no longer being renewed. I went from countless contracts to one. While all of this was going on, I was also enlightened that if I wanted to keep the medical supply company, I'd need to go back to school and obtain multiple certificates. What in the world had just happened? My comfortable world—my entire piece of mind—was crumbling. I'd gone from expeditious spending to depending solely on my husband's income. I was very angry with God, to the point I wanted to walk away from Him. I continued going to church and participated in "churchy stuff," but I was still angry.

"I trust You to supply my needs and this is the thanks I get?" Livid, I tell you! I tried to reason with God. I begged Him to show me my sin; whatever I had done to make him so angry. *Nothing.* He was silent. I performed many tantrums. Still, NOTHING moved Him. Things just got worse; no light at the end of the tunnel, no rainbow and definitely no joy in the morning. Every morning was hard and the nights were harder.

I didn't realize it then, but I was acting arrogantly toward God, as if He owed me something. In my eyes, He was my genie. I just could not fathom why, all of a sudden, He would leave me hanging. He was my Father, and fathers take care of their daughters. My biological father did, at least financially, so I expected my heavenly one to do so as well.

This ugly dry season lasted six years! Maybe I'm just a slow learner, but every time I thought I was going to have a breakthrough, I was let down again. God told me "no" so much, it affected my self-esteem, confidence and my desire to do anything. Fear overtook me. I felt alone and lonely. It appeared that everyone around me was getting what they wanted, making moves toward their destiny, while walking and living on purpose. As for me, I was stuck in a rut and bitter.

I remember in 2010, I was so broke I went into the market with eight dollars to my name. We needed milk, eggs and bread. Since that's all I had enough to buy, I went in on a mission. However, upon entering the market, I heard the spirit say, "*Get a cart.*" In my rebellious mind, I'm thinking, I don't need a cart. But the spirit was so strong that I gave in. I heard the voice again. "*Get what you need and what you want.*"

Without further hesitation, I started to fill my cart. As I was going to the checkout, I wondered who was going to pay for all that stuff. Just as the thought entered my mind, I looked down and saw a beautiful, crisp, fifty-dollar bill on the floor right in front of me. Several people must've walked right by it. I shouted and cried, because my total at checkout came to $32.08. Not only had God given me what I needed, He gave me extra.

I keep the receipt as a reminder that He *will* supply my needs. Despite all my complaining, my mortgage has never gone unpaid. My children have never gone without. My car is still driving like it did fourteen years ago when it was brand new. My marriage is stronger than ever. The problem was never money or things. It was that I determined God's value on my ability to obtain them. Perception can either enlighten you or confine you in a dark place of nothingness, regardless of your lifestyle, rich or poor.

Throughout the years, there were many times God had shown Himself to me, but I felt I still was not getting what it was He wanted me to see. I asked Him often, "What am I missing?" Then I realized I needed to look deeper within. God asked me, "What are your motives for doing what you do?" After several months of soul-searching and journaling, it finally hit me. I was driven by status, fame, money and accolades... not in the typical sense, but in loving to be the one to front the bill in group settings. I have always been a giver by nature, so when I'm not able to, I feel less than myself, like a failure. This season devastated me and I felt destroyed by it, beaten and dead. I had nothing and felt I was nothing. I was lacking relationship. Fortunately for me, whether I praised Him or not, Jesus loved me anyhow. I needed that more than I knew.

My greatest issue was trying to find purpose in tangible desires. Everyone around me appeared content and on a definite road to somewhere. I was defining myself by what I could afford and how much I could give, until I could barely afford groceries for my own household. It was almost as though I couldn't function without receiving some type of praise. The truth is, I was so stuck on being given praise that I forgot to give praise where it mattered most. Friends and family weren't responsible for my success or my lack thereof. And as much as I'd like to think differently, neither was I. It was, and will always be, God.

I watched people around me being promoted in all areas of life. It was borderline sickening how envious I became, simply because I couldn't find contentment in my own world. Living life without purpose is dangerous. Being unable to connect the dots to identify your purpose is fatal.

You don't always know why you are here. It's not spelled out in bold letters across the wall, nor is it walking through your front door each morning to smack you in the face. But if you can recognize what makes you smile inside and out, I mean truly warm you to the depths of your soul, you are on the right path. Passion and purpose are spiritually synonymous.

For me, it's in celebrating life. I get so much joy and pleasure in seeing other people happy. I take pride in being the reason behind someone's smile. For so long I concerned myself with what everyone else had going on, unaware that what God had for me, right before my eyes, was plenty. He hadn't forgotten me or short-changed me.

It took me having to go without to realize His purpose for me is to give, to inspire, to make people feel good and to encourage them to love, despite, because and without condition. After all, that's how God loves us.

On my journey I learned that purpose isn't one size or shape. It's tailored to each of us in different seasons. God does not work on our time. It took years before I experienced my "Aha!" moment, and that's not to be daunting, rather to encourage patience. It's okay to be frustrated sometimes, even angry. It happens. God understands even your angriest prayers. At times when you feel yourself growing covetous because of someone else's blessing, be reminded that God has no favorites. You are exactly where you're supposed to be. When the time comes for you to be promoted, do so humbly.

Don't let monetary things or vanity dictate your status, because in the blink of an eye, it can all be gone. There is nothing wrong with you. God hasn't forgotten you. The nights of crying because you feel all alone, He is right there, watching and listening. It hurts Him to watch His children suffer, but He knows what you will become after the midnight hour.

He knows all. He knows my secret disappointments in life, my secret jealousies of women who can stay at home and not have to work and my longing to live a life where money is not an issue. Right now that is not my reality, and I am okay with that. God knew all of my issues without me uttering one word. He also knew what was best for me. My job is to trust that He will work all things out for my good. Sure, I miss the "good old days" when I was able to splurge more, but I am no longer driven by it. Don't get me wrong, it took some practice. Do I long for those days again? YES! But that is not my motivating factor anymore. My purpose is to teach others how to live and inspire inward heartfelt change. I no longer question His plan for my life. It's scary to think how, when money was everything to me, I craved for people to come to me, needing me. Thank God for clarity and deliverance. I didn't realize until God pried my hands off the situation that *I* was the problem. God created everything purposefully, including me.

All the while I was asking Him questions like, "Why are things not the way *I* wanted? Why am *I* not rich? Why didn't *I* get that promotion? When will *my* day come? God, what about *ME*?" As I stood on my soapbox of rage, angry and self-righteous, shaking my finger in God's face, I should've been thanking Him instead.

In His sovereign grace, wisdom, and above all, His unconditional love for me, I realized that all this time the real question I should've been asking was, "God, what about You?" Once I realized He was not the question, but the answer, I was able to TRULY begin living.

~ Now unto him that is able to do exceeding abundantly above all that we ask or think, according to the power that worketh in us. **Ephesians 3:20 (KJV)**

Chapter 3

The Woman Behind the Hat:

She Doesn't Look Like What She's Been Through

Kimberley Davidson

> "In the midst of the chaos surrounding us, God still has his hands on us and is able to restore us."

Question

Have you ever made a decision outside of the will of God and all hell started to break loose around you, only to realize in hindsight, it was a necessary process?

~3~

Up until 2009, my life was seemingly great on the outside. Everything any one person could possibly want, I had; a huge house, handsome husband and beautiful kids. Little did I know that "picture-perfect" lifestyle would all come crashing down.

My husband and I were living in Miami, Florida where life was grand. We were in the military, he in the Navy, and I in the Air Force. Our finances were substantial, and I was truly in love with a man who loved me back. Basically, our family life had been nothing short of complete. Let the outside world tell it, and that's the story you would get. But it wasn't exactly the truth. Don't get me wrong, like I said before, our finances were better than okay, and I do believe my husband loved me, but never did he verbalize or convey it unless I would say or show it first. Often times I felt as though he didn't tell me he loved me enough. He didn't show me either. We'd talk, but never in a thought provoking way. We didn't do the affectionate things that I'd say normal married couples did. We only hung out when I initiated the idea. He was an introvert, which was okay, except I wanted to do more than sit around on the couch at night and watch movies. Even with our obvious differences, we stayed together.

After two years in Miami, we got word that my husband would be getting orders to Virginia Beach. By the time we moved, I had separated from the Air Force. I decided to explore other passions outside of the military, but my husband was still fully engulfed in serving his country. His new assignment entailed frequent deployments that lasted months at a time, which meant I'd be home alone.

I became the Ombudsman of my husband's command, which is the liaison between the ship while deployed and the families back home. Prior to the first deployment, I met with the Master Chief Petty Officer to discuss my duties and responsibilities as the Ombudsman. I liked the Master Chief right away. He was very real and entertaining. He kept me laughing. After discussing my duties, the Master Chief talked to me about himself and his career. He then went on to share with me that every time he leaves for deployments, he sits down and has a very serious conversation with his wife. He told me he lets her know what he expects of her while he's gone. For example, he expects to hear from her a certain amount of times a day, to get some type of care package, and most importantly, she better not have a man in his house or bed! Deep down inside, I envied his wife for having the type of husband who took the time to tell her how he felt about their marriage and about her as a wife before he deployed.

As he was telling me this, all that was going through my mind was, *That's what I'm talking about!* I yearned for that type of communication from my husband. I wanted him to tell me things like that. I love when a man takes control and lets his woman know she belongs to him and no other man. I don't mean this in a controlling way. I just like to feel wanted and that he loves me so much that he doesn't want anyone else to have what he has…me.

After meeting with the Master Chief, I told my husband all about the conversation, particularly the conversations the Master Chief has with his wife before deploying. My husband laughed and said the Master Chief was hilarious. Yeah, he was a very funny man; however, his conversations with his wife were very real and important to have. He had been in the Navy for many years and had seen and been through some things, so he knew what needed to be discussed in a marriage.

As my husband prepared to go on the first deployment with this command, I waited to receive a conversation with him regarding what he expected of me while he was deployed. That conversation never happened. I know some people may think that its common sense and that I should know what and what not to do, and I did. I just wanted to hear from my husband's mouth that I meant the world to him and that he loved his family and wanted me to hold everything down while he was away. I think real conversations go a long way, at least with me they do.

During the times he was away, I relied heavily on our kids and school to occupy my time. Thankfully, I was able to snag an internship with a bridal show production company that kept me nice and busy. In the process, I was tasked with many duties, particularly holding casting calls for models. That's where I met "him." For the sake of anonymity, I'll just refer to him as "Ole Boy."

Ole Boy was funny, charming, had a relationship with the Lord, was strikingly handsome, and he gave me all the attention I was missing from my husband. I didn't have many friends in the area, so he really filled a void.

It was put out there early on that the both of us already had significant others, so the relationship we formed was strictly casual. Crossing the lines was something we were determined not to do.

After six months had gone by, my husband finally returned from his first deployment. Before I could even get comfortable with having him around, he was preparing to leave again. I was so exhausted with the back and forth, not to mention it was around the holidays. We sat around playing cards and eating. I guess we were supposed to be having family time prior to his leaving, but I was so bored. I mean *really* bored. At one point during our family time I ended up excusing myself to go into the home office to make a call on my cellphone.

Ole Boy became my entertainment, relieving me from boredom. For the next two hours, we texted back and forth, discussing no one thing in particular. But he'd done what he did best, which was to make me laugh. I thought it was so odd that he could keep my attention more than the man who I'd decided to share my life with, the one that was literally feet away from me, preparing to leave me alone for however many more months.

I don't know if I was just frustrated with my circumstances or simply jaded. What I did know was that the more I communicated with Ole Boy, the more I started to invest interest in him outside of just being casual. In fact, the day after my husband left, Ole Boy and I were in contact.

I had an upcoming trip about a month out and told Ole Boy I needed a ride to the airport. I really didn't need a ride. I could have driven myself even. But it was an opportunity for me to see and spend a little time with him. He agreed to drop me off, but as the date neared, he became reluctant. I think he had been expecting us to be at another level by then. Maybe he wanted us to have had sex by that point, because he kept saying things like, "Well, you're married anyway." That was my first hint to bow out gracefully. Unfortunately, I didn't take heed.

I convinced him to still come and pick me up to take me to the airport. We began chatting even more than before. Finally, after all this conversing, we decided to go to dinner together. This had been awkward for so many reasons, the obvious being that I was married. Come to think of it, he'd been the first man I'd been out with, other than my husband, since I had been married. To make matters more uncomfortable, instead of sitting across from me at dinner, he wanted to sit next to me. I insisted that he did not.

Despite my apprehensions, I allowed one thing to lead to another. What Ole Boy and I had certainly started to feel like something more than just a friendship. It was *so* bad, but so good at the same time.

I distinctively remember the time I started getting deep into my affair and two friends took me out to dinner for an intervention. One of them reminded me that what I was involved in was wrong and that the Lord would only throw me life jackets (a way out) but so many times. Boy do I wish I had taken heed to that intervention.

I heard every word they said and agreed with them 100% but at the time, it was like I was having an out of body experience. It was like someone else had taken over my body and I couldn't control them. I could see and hear all the wrong I was doing but for some reason I could not stop!

I couldn't even stop after one day of going to watch Ole Boy and his best friend play basketball. During a break, Ole Boy came over to get something from his bag and out falls a condom! He tried to give me some lame excuse that all men carry condoms even if they aren't using them. Okay, he must have thought I was Boo Boo the Fool or somebody. That was the most ridiculous thing I had ever heard.

I was very quiet for the rest of that evening. I started thinking about what I, someone who was educated, beautiful family, and wanted for nothing was doing in that situation and why I was letting Ole Boy play me. Still knowing that there was a big chance that he was sleeping with someone else, I continued to be with him. I guess one could say, I was playing myself.

I was really struggling with doing the right thing which was ending the affair. I was a Woman of God. I believed in God and truly wanted to do the right thing but after the intervention didn't work and several attempts of my own didn't work, I reached out to my Bishop. I told him about my husband being deployed all the time and not feeling appreciated and I told him about the affair I was having and that I needed help to stop it.

My flesh was weak. I told him that I was in a soul tie with the other guy and I was having trouble breaking free of it. My Bishop's response was so simple and straight forward. He said, "Remove yourself from that person." I don't know what kind of response I was expecting from him but it would have been nice to get a little more meat and potatoes. Maybe I was expecting him to have talked to me in depth about soul ties and consequences that follow them. Removing myself from the person was easier said than done. If it was that simple for me to do, I would have done it however; it was very difficult.

After hearing from my Bishop, I have to admit that I was somewhat crushed. I really wanted help breaking free from the bondage I was in and when I didn't get the response I was hoping for, I literally didn't know what else to do.

While my husband was still out on deployment, he eventually questioned me about this mysterious number that appeared all over our phone bill at all times of the day and night. I'd been on such a high that I hadn't thought about that detail. I told him it was an old friend from my hometown. Surprisingly, he didn't trip about it. To the average person, it definitely would have raised a red flag. I guess, though, my husband trusted me. He knew me to be faithful so it was easy for him to believe my lies. I started to worry about just how long he would continue to believe me. That was another sign to stop while I was ahead. But, I just kept right on...full speed!

I had so many warnings. I had a dear friend from back home in Houston try and talk me out of dealing with Ole Boy. She had known me for many years and couldn't understand how in the world I could get caught up in a situation with someone like him. I knew! I had taken my focus off the Lord and got sucked into a world that I was not ready nor prepared for.

He was not the typical guy I would give my time to. Yes, he was good looking but ordinarily it would take more than good looks to get my attention. My friend knew from the very beginning that Ole Boy was not good for me. And when I told her he was an Aries, she really went in to get me to leave him alone.

I am not in tuned with all of the astronomy and signs and such but I will say that she was on point with Ole Boy and all of his shenanigans.

I'll never forget the day my husband returned home after his second deployment. I took the kids to greet him at the terminal, which was understandably a big deal in the military world. You know, your husband has been gone for however long, and the first thing he wants to see when he steps onto land is his family. And so there we stood as he walked over wearing his crisp uniform and a smile as wide as the ocean. Naturally, he leaned in to kiss me—his wife--and I turned my face away. Yikes! If that hadn't been hurtful enough, when he tried to hold my hand, I pulled mine away. I resisted anything that involved him touching me. What was going through my head to be so cold and inconsiderate, I can't say. But in hindsight, I cringe at the thought.

I couldn't distinguish if guilt was driving my actions or something else. There was an undeniable disconnect in my marriage. Things would get worse before getting better.

Since my husband was now home, Ole Boy began to worry that we'd be found out. In agitation, my only reply was, "If it comes out, just blame it on me." He seemed content with that option. Well, the mess did hit the fan. Apparently when my husband wasn't busy being a Navy Officer, he'd had a side job as Inspector Gadget. When I say he found everything from phone bills to receipts, I tell no lies. How he was able to conjure up all that information, I still couldn't say for sure, but when he confronted the other man in my life, things went left.

Never did I think Ole Boy would actually blame everything on me, but he did! Man, talk about a coward. He led my husband to believe that I'd never mentioned being married. At this point I was beyond shocked. The way I saw it was, hey, we're *both* caught. Either keep your mouth shut or be a man and own up to your part. I guess that was my fault for expecting more from this guy.

Be that as it may, my husband cared enough to try and work things out in our marriage. But silly me continued dealing with Ole Boy. I was so confused about what I wanted and about what I didn't want. I just know that despite my husband's diligent attempts to save our marriage, it was Ole Boy I craved.

I'd never considered leaving my husband for this man. Some of my friends and a friend of his would say that the two of us were in a relationship because we did things that people in a relationship would do. I denied it. I justified my stance by saying, "How can I be in a relationship with him when I'm married?" But honestly, I really did identify what we had as a relationship. I was afraid to admit it and say it out loud because I felt people would think I was crazy. My mind was so twisted; it felt as though I was cheating on my lover with my own husband. I was outside of myself, truly a piece of work.

At one point, I even had the nerve to be a little jealous. One day I was going through Ole Boy's closet to help him pick out something to wear and I came across a dress hanging in the closet. He told me it belonged to his ex and that she had left it there and he never bothered to return it. I remained calm but on the inside I was boiling!

Really Kim….that was the thought I was fighting with inside my head. How could I feel some type of way about what he was doing on the side and I was in a marriage? My flesh took over and I grabbed the dress from the closet, put it up in front of Ole Boy, looked at it and said, "She actually wore this in public?" Ole boy got upset with my comment, rightfully so. There was no need to attack someone I didn't know. It wasn't her I wanted to hurt, it was Ole Boy.

I did feel horrible about what I said and that should have been another time for me to realize I was too involved in my twisted affair.

I thought it was mindboggling that my husband never asked any questions like why I'd cheated on him. He'd been quick to jump into bed with me, which was really irritating, because contrary to my blatant infidelity, I yearned for a resolution. I wanted us as husband and wife to figure out where things had gone wrong. When he didn't ask questions or try to figure out why I was being unfaithful, it felt like my husband didn't really love me. This made my stomach turn.

I figured my outlandish actions had stemmed from the suppressed memory of him cheating with multiple women during our engagement. There was this toxic regimen of resentment residing inside me that hadn't quite been dealt with. I'd been faithful for eleven years before I was unfaithful. My husband wasn't to blame completely, but I did feel a sense of entitlement; that he owed it to me to discuss and get to the bottom of things. How could we ever know for sure without communication?

He did recommend counseling, but by then I was no longer feeling it, so I declined. Meanwhile, I was still messing with Ole Boy. All of a sudden, here comes several mornings of sickness. All that'd been done in the dark was coming to the light. I could no longer tiptoe in the shadows of my reality.

My husband was, again, deployed and I struggled with the idea of telling him such a bludgeoning truth. On the other hand, waiting would only make it worse. So, the next time he called, I told him the hardest thing I'd ever had to say in my entire life; that I was pregnant by someone other than him.

"Congratulations," he said. It wasn't said sarcastically either. He said it as if he was truly wishing me well.

My mouth dropped I was so stunned. I chalked his response up to him not knowing what else to say. He was rightfully devastated and I sure as heck couldn't blame him. Even so, his voice was mellow.

Days later, we spoke again. This time my husband had a proposition; that I not keep the baby if I wanted to keep him. He hadn't been the only one who had made this suggestion. I had a really good friend tell me the same thing and I totally understood why. I already knew what it felt like to be a mother at this point, so having an abortion just wasn't something I would have been able to live with. Against all odds, I went forth with the pregnancy.

Well, I jumped that hurdle to slam into yet another brick wall. Guess who else didn't want me to keep the baby? The father. He fed me this mess about him already having kids. I did too, so what? I knew my decision to keep the baby wouldn't be a walk in the park, but I felt like I'd had plenty of opportunities to get out of the situation beforehand and didn't. I continued to do what I wanted to do instead, and as a result, I ended up pregnant. I needed to take responsibility for my actions. Not only that, but as messed up as my situation was, the bottom line was that I was starting to fall in love with the baby growing inside of me.

Eventually, Ole Boy got over the initial shock factor and decided he'd support my decision, or so he said. The next thing I knew, here I was in the middle of a separation and pregnant by this other man, who, out of nowhere, wanted nothing to do with me or the child I was carrying...*his* child. Needless to say, he remained absent most of my pregnancy. Even while this was taking place, I still felt some kind of obligation to call him when I went into labor. I already knew he and I wouldn't be anything more, but him being a father was different. To my surprise, he showed up to witness his son's birth. When he showed up, he made a big scene as I was being rolled into the delivery room.

The doctor would only allow two hospital bracelets to be made that would give the recipient access to the baby twenty-four hours. I had one and I instructed the doctor to give the other one to a friend of mine because she was staying at the hospital with me while I was in recovery. I knew the father wouldn't stick around after the birth, so why waste a twenty-four hour bracelet on him? Well, he demanded the other bracelet go to him.

I threw in the towel. At that moment all I could think about was that my baby was being born a month and a half early due to complications. I was scared to death and all he wanted to do was argue about a hospital bracelet.

A little over a year passed after the birth of the baby. At this point I essentially had nothing. My husband and I were separated and my baby's father had become a person who I no longer knew. I had some income coming in, but I wasn't working, so financially, I was no longer comfortable. My husband still took care of our two kids together, so I didn't have to worry there. But I was raising this new baby alone. The father was questioning paternity, which was completely ridiculous being that he showed up at the hospital to see his son born. He'd even signed the birth certificate documents. Because I was still legally married, though, the state wouldn't put his name on the actual birth certificate. That stalled child support for months. This was the beginning of the foolishness I would have to go through with Ole Boy.

The situation I found myself in was devastating to say the least. After losing things that were dear to me, I also had to endure feelings of loneliness and abandonment from someone I had once considered a friend. I had done so much for him (willingly), and thought he somewhat cared about me. Clearly that wasn't the case.

After everything hit the fan, I was fine with him and me not being involved anymore. What I wasn't prepared for was his resentment toward myself and the son we had together. His actions made me feel like I was being sucker punched in the face and kicked in the stomach.

Even if we were never going to be involved again, I just wanted him to do right by his child. He chose not to, for whatever reason, and that caused some issues that I still currently face.

Fundamentally, I lost my family. I mean, if it was ever mine to claim, I'd lost it. People who I thought would stand by me no matter what turned their backs. At one point, I didn't know who I could turn to or trust. There was no loyalty. No one was communicating directly with me. Instead, they talked amongst themselves trying to figure out what I should have done as if they knew better than me. They knew bits and pieces of what had transpired, but not the entire situation. I felt as though I was being judged by the mistakes I'd made as if no one else had ever made any.

Some days I didn't see how I would make it...but God! That experience has definitely drawn me closer to the Lord. As hurtful as this process has been, I'm glad I now have a stronger relationship with Christ. Who knows? Maybe it took that experience for this to happen. Either way, I'm grateful. I am also thankful that the process has allowed me to grow as a woman and to learn some things about myself, such as the amazing strength I have that enabled me to endure everything with grace and integrity. To God be the glory for this not breaking me but making me stronger!

What I feel most terrible about in my situation is how I hurt my husband. This man truly loved me. If I didn't know it before, I know it now just by how he has dealt with me since this whole ordeal occurred. I don't know any man who would tolerate me after what I did. This man still cared and did things for me and the child born to me outside our marriage. Even if we never reconcile, I am forever grateful to this man.

I would give anything to have all that I once had restored back; my joy, peace, my family. I can't turn back the hands of time. All I can do is learn from my mistakes and continue to fulfill my purpose.

Through my journey I have learned that when you make mistakes and think they are unforgivable, don't give up on Jesus. When the people who claim to love and care about you turn their backs and betray you and your trust, don't give up on Jesus. When you don't see a light at the end of your tunnel, don't give up on Jesus. When people confuse your faith with being crazy/craziness, don't give up on Jesus.

I think as Christians, especially women, we place distinct obligations on ourselves, then spend our entire lives trying to see them through. The most important, yet forgotten, are the ones we think come easily: to follow your heart, be virtuous, and do whatever brings peace and happiness to yourself and those around you. But we often forget that we are human, which means we are imperfect and flawed. In our best intentions, we are never exempt from making mistakes. However, God is faithful. Even in my lowest, loneliest moments, He was the ONLY one I could count on to keep me in my right mind. Everything I had, which wasn't necessarily tangible, He had provided. Peace, direction, the ability to see my children smile—all things required to make it through my days. Sound restoration. Faults and all, God's love for me did not alter.

I learned the hard way that people can't take old things and make them new again. They can't take broken hearts and make them whole. But He can, and He did. I am the living proof.

Not too many people are aware of what I have gone through. I don't think they'd believe me if I told them. All they see is a well dressed woman with a beautiful smile who seems to have it all together but, behind the *Hats* I wear is a woman who has been broken; and written across my face are words of shame, disappointment, guilt, hurt and regret. I definitely don't look like what I've been through.

The unfolding of the process I went through has given me insight as to what my purpose is in helping to expand the Kingdom. I am now introducing an initiative to speak the truth about soul ties and restoration. I now know that I was deeply in bondage in a soul tie with Ole Boy. As a result, I want to help women who struggle with all types of ungodly soul ties and help them break the bondage they are in and put them on the road to restoration.

My story is still being written, lived, and fought through. It is far from over, believe me, so stay tuned. But I can tell you in advance that victory is already mine and that I thank God for!

~ 6 "'Nevertheless, I will bring health and healing to it; I will heal my people and will let them enjoy abundant peace and security. 7 I will bring Judah and Israel back from captivity and will rebuild them as they were before. 8 I will cleanse them from all the sin they have committed against me and will forgive all their sins of rebellion against me. 9 Then this city will bring me renown, joy, praise and honor before all nations on earth that hear of all the good things I do for it; and they will be in awe and will tremble at the abundant prosperity and peace I provide for it.'

10 "This is what the LORD says: 'You say about this place, "It is a desolate waste, without people or animals." Yet in the towns of Judah and the streets of Jerusalem that are deserted, inhabited by neither people nor animals, there will be heard once more 11 the sounds of joy and gladness, the voices of bride and bridegroom, and the voices of those who bring thank offerings to the house of the LORD, saying, "Give thanks to the LORD Almighty, for the LORD is good; his love endures forever." For I will restore the fortunes of the land as they were before,' says the LORD. **Jeremiah 33:6-11 (NIV)**

Chapter 4

A Polished Woman:
Still Standing

Kimberly Jenkins

> "So many marriages fail and with that, often times it seems like the person you call spouse and thought you married is not the person that you thought they were at all."

Question

How many brides plan their wedding and a divorce at the same time to the same man?

~4~

Every day I showed up. Not a hair on my head was out of place. I may have cried all the way there and again on the way home, but publicly, I remained poised. Dental Hygienist was what had been stamped on my acceptance form to Northern Virginia Community College, and I was determined to finish as such. It may have seemed backward to most because I had already obtained my B.S. in Marketing from Hampton University. Yet, I always wanted a career in the dental field. However, if I ever had any desire for a career switch, acting would have been a distinct possibility. I mean, I could really turn my emotions on and off.

Routinely, before class I'd check *it* at the door—fix my face, change into my scrubs, find my smile. Allowing anyone to see me less than together was not happening. In spite of the way I felt, I flourished through my courses with my head held high. Both teachers and fellow students adored me. My grades were always above average, as was my pleasant attitude. If I would have told you my life was not perfect, you never would have believed me.

Well, it wasn't. In fact, it was far from it. I was so stressed outside of school, that I craved being there, just to have some temporary peace. My home was what I liked to call a "pretty prison." The exterior was quaint. From the curb, one could look at the house and think of how warm and inviting it might be. It was perfectly located in a great area in a very sought after Northern Virginia development. Yet, when you stepped inside, there was this instant chill factor. By definition it was unquestionably a house, but it was far from a home. I didn't feel warm or comforted. I felt trapped. Not literally, of course, because at any moment, the option to turn around and walk out the door was there. Even so, with a husband I barely recognized as the same man I'd fallen in love with and married, and now a fulltime student without my own income anymore, how the heck could I go anywhere?

The truth was, what remained of my marriage was crumbling. I'd already seen signs beforehand. In 1999, after delivering beautiful twin boys, I figured any man would be over the top with joy. We'd already had a beautiful little girl and were now blessed with two boys to carry on the family name. After relocating from Maryland to our beautiful home in Herndon, VA, one of the twins was diagnosed with reflux. Prior to his diagnosis, he was fussy, especially after having a bottle. The only exception was if I laid him against my bosom and fed him "liquid gold," which was breast milk of course. He would remain settled and I could get some relief.

One day, as his father held him, he began to get fussy. Knowing my husband had worked all day, I quickly put my other son down and went to assist. As soon as I got close, he tossed the baby into my hands and exclaimed, "Take this whiny momma's boy!"

I caught my baby without thought as if I'd known what was about to happen. Call it a mother's instinct or a mother's worse nightmare. I stood in shock and felt the tears forming. I had seen this side of him before, but it was usually directed toward me.

Life continued and the kids began to grow older and more independent. Our marital disagreements were usually, for him, about lack of intimacy. For me it was money and the kids. No matter what it was, though, everything was always my fault. He had an uncanny way of turning everything around and blaming me—even for events that happened to him at work. He would call me out of my name, especially when he began to drink. The more he hung out after work drinking, the more altercations there were between the two of us.

One Christmas he was annoyed with me because I'd asked him to hang our Christmas lights so my father wouldn't have to drive up four hours to hang them for his grandchildren. He stormed out of the house, putting up a huge fuss, but he did eventually go outside to hang them. I actually felt guilty for asking him to do it, so I went outside to where he was and asked if he wanted me to fix him a drink. Yes, a drink. Even though God knows that was his poison, I just wanted to get on his good side so that we could perhaps have an okay evening.

He turned and looked at me and said, "You know, you're a great mother but a terrible wife."

Wow! I did not feel the knife from that sharp comment coming for my stomach. Not realizing that I was really about to start a major spiritual battle that would last for years to come, I did what I did best back then, cry in our bathroom so the kids couldn't see or hear me. And I prayed. Still the words he spoke to me that day continued to resonate in my head, even after things went back to our dysfunctional normal, if you will. Even worse, I was really beginning to believe the cruel things he would say to me.

I started questioning myself; my worth and my purpose. In the midst of it all, my discernment was getting sharper and my responses became less argumentative and all about finding the true cause of his actions, which included his drinking, unexplained after work functions and occasional disappearances. I felt part of the truth was the fact that he was becoming an alcoholic, although he denied it or minimized it. I would collect his liquor store receipts as well as his bottles of alcohol he was plowing through and put them in big mall size shopping bags. I might have needed them for proof of his abusive tendencies, not to mention to prove I wasn't over exaggerating his drinking habits. I stored them at a neighbor's house so that he wouldn't discover what I was doing. He was a quiet man, so to the world he seemed like a gentle giant. But to me, and eventually others, he had another side — a dark, angry side.

I had the best neighbors in the world. They always had my back even with carpooling our kids to and from activities or arranging play dates so I could simply run errands. One couple had witnessed some unsettling exchanges between my husband and me. They came to my home together one evening and gave me a key to their house. They told me anytime the kids and I needed to come to their home, the door was open. They wanted me to know we had somewhere safe to go.

It wasn't too long after that when the same couple came to me again with some news. They knew I'd been worried about where my husband was. He'd had a meeting in DC earlier, but he should have long been home. They told me they'd passed him coming down Route 7, a major street by our house, which was nowhere near DC. That wasn't the half of it though. They'd seen him with another woman—a white woman. My mind immediately went back to a dream that had awakened me out of my sleep one night. It was so real that I couldn't fall back to sleep. In my dream, he was involved with another woman. I couldn't see her face, but I knew she was white. Her ethnicity in my dream probably derived from the many inferences he'd made against blacks, more specifically, black women. I don't know to this day where the self-hatred came from— Black parents, Black grandmother, sister, daughter, sons— but he didn't like his own people. He went as far as telling me that he would never deal with another black woman again. That statement was clearly a sign that he was looking, but not a sign I was ready to admit.

How did he think this would make his African American children feel if they ever heard him say that?

I felt in my spirit that dream with him and the Caucasian woman was God preparing me for what was to come. I had only had such vivid and realistic dreams a few times, but they'd all been accurate in what came to pass. The dreams were like double edged swords. I wanted signs that reflected the honest truth about my marriage, but dealing with the truth is something altogether different than just hearing it.

Eyes Wide Open and Reflecting

By the next Christmas holiday, my favorite time of the year, he moved out of our home, *one week before Christmas,* taking some clothes and a few of his personal items. Prior to his move he'd made several trips to California to see his best friend. After abandoning us, I found bank statements reflecting his generous spending at high end hotel stays while in California. Here he'd told me he was staying with his best friend. On most occasions, according to my careful scanning of our bank statements, he had not.

Upon my discovery, I called him up to inform him of my findings. He lied and denied, got angry and did his usual; started spewing cruel words and heavy venom at me as if I had done something to him.

After that, when he would go out of town, my calls would not get answered and he never even called to check on our kids. Surely his kids and I deserved better than that. I wanted to throw in the towel, but I was taught to hang in there and make it work. I had watched so many people I love fight for their marriages, so surely I could do it as well.

My parents were so supportive, as were his. I didn't want to disappoint them or tear up our families. But I got tired of appearing one way to the world and living in a hell within my home. Things were so bad that some friends of ours came to the house to pray over it. Now this is where faith really started kicking in. I started believing if I prayed for him with a pure heart and not malice, God would turn this thing around. In between the trips to California, alcohol, mental abuse and the 911 calls I'd made out of fear for myself and the children, I prayed.

He's Back

In February 2007, I allowed him to come back home, however, I slept in the bedroom and he slept in the basement. He might not have been sharing a bed with me, but I wasn't alone. I slept with a knife under my mattress. I just didn't feel like I knew the man I'd married anymore, let alone what he was capable of. I continued to pray.

I read a book called *Power of a Praying Wife* and had the epiphany that this book was written because so many women had to endure a lot of what I was going through. Ironically, the book instructed me to pray for my husband—accountability and praying with a pure heart. That was something I was already doing of course. But what a challenge it was, because I felt like the victim. Clearly there were some things God wanted me to learn about myself during this process. I knew I was doing something right because it seemed like the harder I prayed, the harder the enemy went to work.

Picking my kids up from aftercare, I was greeted by one of the teachers. She pulled me aside. I knew immediately what she wanted to address. The night before, my husband had the kids with him and that same baby he'd tossed into my arms, he had struck "accidentally" and gashed him under the eye, causing a bruise. My son, who was five years old at the time, asked me in front of his dad, "What if the school asks what happened to my eye?"

I stooped down and looked my baby in his glassy eyes and responded, "You do what mommy has always taught you to do—tell the truth."

You can mess with me, but I'll be *doggone* if

you're going to mistreat my babies. Even with a fear of my kids possibly being taken away, I informed the teacher that their father had caused the bruise, but it was an accident. That night when my children went to sleep—as with many other nights—I laid in each of their rooms on the floor crying. This was so unfair to them. Why couldn't they have the happy family I'd seen so many people have—that I had as a child. Why couldn't they experience family dinners together where their father actually sat down at the table, consistently showing them affection and not just when things went his way and the moon and stars were in perfect alignment. They deserved more and I did too.

In hindsight, I didn't have a clue as to how the entire time God was really covering me and my children. How?

The Blessings

Well, one of many things I can site is the fact that he never came upstairs and bothered us, except for the night I finally had him served with divorce papers. That night I had one child still awake and shaking from the way his father was yelling and screaming at me. Once again I found myself on the phone with a 911 operator. She told me to stay on the phone and asked if I felt the other kids were safe. I knew they were asleep. If I could just take this one and get out of the house, he would eventually pass out in a drunken stupor. I did manage to do just that, so the police ended up not coming out that time. But after that, they came even on the occasion when I called 911 and hung up without summoning them.

Not only did God send the police to my aid on several occasions, but He sent angels galore. The assistant principal of my children's school knew I needed someone to watch my children during this one particular semester where I had to see patients in the evenings once per week. She offered to not only take them home after school, but fed them and helped them get their homework done. Wow! Thank you God! As if that hadn't been enough to make me shout, my daughter's tutor, who came to our home to tutor her once a week, called me one morning. She told me that she could sense something was going on in the home and had noticed that my husband was a heavy drinker. She told me that if I ever needed her to speak to that matter in court, she would. Talk about God seeing to it that somebody had my back!

God had been putting blessings in place via my children's teachers long before that. Who knew that the preschool my daughter once attended would also be the source of another angel and lifetime friend? The owner of the school was a God-fearing, strong, and loving person who provided another safe haven. She and her sister prayed for me when I got tired of crying and praying for myself. She even offered to let my twins go to her preschool as long as I watched all of the kids at nap time and helped answer the phones so she could run errands. With me there her teachers could still have a go-to person in the office in her absence. This was the same person who would later come to my rescue the night I found out my husband was taking another trip to California after having caught him sneaking out at three in the morning to catch his flight.

This particular incident occurred the week I had exams. I was at my wit's end. How was I going to get through my exams while trying to care for three children by myself? I was going through a divorce and taking an exam in the one class that I was struggling to pass. In hygiene school, anything less than a "C" was considered failing. My friend who owned the preschool came to my home and she picked me up off of the floor, sat me on my couch and prayed for me while I wept. She looked at me and said, "You will take this exam and you will get some rest. Go upstairs. I'll stay here while you sleep and I'll get the kids ready for school and drop them off."

Wow again, right! I remember crying through my exam. It was the end of my two long, hard years. My professor happened to be the doctor on staff for our hygiene class. He also attended the same church as my kids' assistant principal. His class was the one class I was struggling in. He watched me cry for the first time while taking the final exam. He called me up after I turned in my test. He had me stand there while he graded it. I watched red marks flowing continuously from pen to paper as he marked all of my wrong answers. He then turned to me and said, "You failed my exam, Ms. Jenkins, but you passed my class." That's called FAVOR!

Do you see God all in this thing or what? In the midst of all of this craziness, my storm was actually chock full of blessings, and more to come that I was oblivious to. I might add that I had lost over 32 pounds (the D (divorce)-Diet—not recommended but totally effective). The man who told me that no one was going to want a woman with three kids and about to turn 40 had no idea how many men I was having to fight off.

My lawyer had given me very strict instructions to make sure I didn't do anything he could use against me. I had an open and shut case. I would be lying to you if I told you it didn't feel great to have compliments flying left and right and not someone pouring negative thoughts into my head. But I refused to allow the devil to use any type of distractions to get me off course.

Needless to say, I knew the end was near. After 11 years of marriage, this was a scary thought. This was not about just me. I was going to have to be everything for my kids; the bread winner, mother, cook, tutor, driver, confidante, protector. Wait! Hadn't I pretty much been doing that all along? But this time, I had to make sure they were in a healthy, loving environment. My biggest concern was how I'd be able to survive financially on my own. I was afraid of starting all over.

As to be expected, I had a lot of emotions, but was determined my focus had to be my kids and how I planned to provide for them. Finishing school would be my means of doing so. In the meantime, since I was a fulltime student without income, leaving didn't seem smart. Staying with a man who'd clearly thrown in the towel with me wasn't going to work either. This is where the prison set in. I'd been kept in the dark for so long with finances, I felt as though I was being held hostage inside my own home.

It was surreal how much control I *thought* I didn't have over my own life. Ironically, although I coined school as my safe haven, I seldom mentioned my situation to anyone there. Even so, I was constantly being told stories by patients I treated and classmates. Their stories were similar to mine, but ten times worse. I figured if this woman is going through this and still smiling, then I can do this. I can get through my situation.

Meanwhile, a fellow student and dear friend of mine suggested I run for class president. Picture that! In the midst of all the adversity going on in my world, I was still being called to leadership. I politely declined, knowing I had way too much on my plate as it was. I did, however, run for vice-president. Effortlessly, I obtained the position.

While vice president, I laughed, I bonded with everyone, I engulfed myself in positivity. Then, at the end of each day, I'd get in my car to drive home, no longer crying, but spilling over with anxiety. Just before I'd put the key in the door, my stomach would turn to knots. I mean, instant queasiness, because I knew what faced me on the other side. I had to cook and study, which already called for long nights. I'd gotten used to that much. But the root of my distress was the fear I'd developed—can I really do this on my own? I was now going to be solely responsible for three little people's lives. But the knot in the pit of my stomach was slowly but surely starting to go away.

Experiencing divorce is tough, but doing so while living under the same roof as the soon-to-be ex-spouse is almost unbearable, especially when there are kids— young ones—around to witness it. Indeed, he was my husband, but he was their father. I needed him back to normal, more for their sake than my own. Yet and still, as the man I vowed to love forever continued to allow alcohol to transform him into someone I could now barely recognize, I prayed for a way out.

The Real Separation Begins

To protect myself, at night I'd locked the door to the bedroom. In the evenings, I hosted study groups at my house so that I wouldn't be alone. The rest of the time I relied heavily on my outside support system. I pretty much had the safety issue covered. Then the bills stopped getting paid. Now I was terrified. The only income I'd had was from student loans, which didn't stretch very far. My husband had been the breadwinner for the latter part of our marriage. All of a sudden, we're down to crumbs. No, I was. He was doing just fine.

At this point, even though we were still sharing residency, I was responsible for my own bills. I had family and friends willing to help, but I'd already bothered them enough with my day-to-day problems. I didn't want to wear them out with my financial baggage too. I did my best to make it work as much as I could without help.

Besides school, church became instrumental to my sanity. I started attending a fairly larger church than what I'd been used to. It had roughly 3,000 members at that time. The music was contemporary and moving, and the people were warm and friendly. It was a no-brainer...this was a good place of refuge for the kids and me.

I went on to join the choir, inadvertently landing the role as a lead singer. This was important to me, because while I managed to keep it together on the outside, I was still experiencing the worst time of my life. I had always been successful in everything I'd done, so to have a marriage that wasn't going to make it, to me, was the epitome of failure.

Daily, I clung onto two things: the comradery of the community surrounding me, and going to Friday night choir rehearsals. *This* was home for me. It was a place where I could truly relax in an atmosphere of unconditional love. It was almost like a football team, the way we all played our parts in being there for one another. We'd huddle together, pray powerful prayers, then get up there and sing like our lives depended on it. Each of us had some kind of burden plaguing us, but we were able to counter it by joining as a unit and doing what we were called to do. I had no idea how the years of support I got from that group would play a role in my life. God specifically sent them to me—or me to them. Either way, there is no one person alive that could ever convince me otherwise.

My life had become a complicated, secretive juggling act that I'd learned to master with a smile; the good, the bad and the ugly. Inside, I was so torn up. But my Perfect Patty mask was flawless, so much so, that it wasn't until just before I graduated that anyone, outside of my circle, noticed my underlying scars. My Jack and Jill chapter, my daughter's brownie troop, people at the church (aside from the choir), and most family had not been privy to the weak and scared side of me. Clearly, my gut wrenching, hearty laugh, hair, makeup and nails would mask what was really going on.

The one person I truly couldn't hide from was my mother. I called her crying quite often, but even then I didn't want her to worry, so I held back the gritty details. My dad only knew what I allowed him to know because I feared he would call in the Texas Calvary (cousins and uncles). Things would get real ugly then. I did what I had to do and covered what I had to cover to protect my children. They were my motivation for all I did.

Even though my husband and I occupied separate living quarters in the home, unfortunately that didn't stop the arguing and fighting or the police from frequenting the property. To say my living situation was unhealthy would be an understatement. It was hell. My safety was constantly at risk, and while I never felt my children were physically in harm's way, today, I believe, emotionally it was damaging and I should have removed them from that environment long before I did.

It saddens me to think how long I stayed in that house before light was finally shed upon my situation. I'd been hospitalized on several occasions due to stress-induced migraines, but I didn't leave. I was abandoned for days and even months and forced to be the bearer of bad news to my children—that their father had moved out. Yes, he had left me to do the explaining.

All in all, no matter how low, hurtful or harmful

my circumstances, I remembered one thing: to praise God always, because on the other side, I knew something greater awaited me.

Through praising Him (notice I didn't say begging Him), I was able to receive all the necessary resources to hurl myself to a place of independency. I was blessed with a community of support that I will always be grateful for. The assistant principal of my kids' school watched them voluntarily when my schedule changed. I had keys to one of my neighbor's homes, which I deemed our safe house in the event of an emergency. I had a girlfriend who owned a school that I was blessed to work at long enough to get my own children through school.

Even after the school closed, she still extended an offer to help me with the kids as much as I needed. In addition, I was able to meet individuals, from lawyers to friends, who enabled me to handle my divorce confidently and with competence. The list goes on and on. Amidst what most would deem havoc, I took as a lesson learned. I learned my rights as a wife, but more importantly, as a faithful, praying Christian.

Finalizing my divorce was like cartwheeling across just one finish line of a seemingly never-ending marathon of life. The hardest part was already over. This wasn't a failure anymore. It was confirmation to start the process of healing.

I won't lie and say transitioning from unhappily ever after wasn't the longest, most draining journey I've ever had to endure. What I will say is this; having internal peace was so worth the battle. I was relieved in knowing my children and I could finally exhale. Repainting the tainted family portrait would take some work, but that would come with time. God had already brought me through hell. Why wouldn't I believe He could restore the other areas of my life?

In all honesty, if I thanked Him a trillion times, it still would not be enough. I am so much better now. I'll never forget the nights that I cried more than I prayed or even the nights I prayed more than I cried. My test is the very reason I find myself crying tears of joy now. Our storms teach us to appreciate sunshine, and I have plenty!

I am happy. There's no simpler way to say it. I don't feel like a prisoner in my own home, or inside my own head. As much as I hated the process, I had to go through it to get here. And now I have a passion to travel and minister to women by doing speaking engagements, using the radio as an opportunity to share my testimony, in the grocery store or whenever I see someone who "appears" like I did while going through. I simply lend an ear or advice if sought. But God always gets the glory. ALWAYS!!!

My support system is still as imperative now as it

was in my time of turmoil. The fact that I didn't have all the pieces of this crazy puzzle figured out, but I was still embraced anyhow, lets me know God is real. He's been with me all along. Praise and you shall receive abundantly.

My once broken heart is renewed. My smile, once forced, is equally as genuine as it is contagious (God didn't put me in the dentistry field for nothing *wink*). Side note—I remarried the most wonderful man, a dentist ironically, who I had actually known since college. He is a great father and even better husband, and ladies, I wasn't even looking. God sent him to me!

The light makeup I throw on every now and then is but a complement to my natural beauty, radiating from inside out. In essence, I feel as good as I look. All the bumps and bruises along the way were necessary.

Scarred, scorned and strengthened—I am the definition of a polished woman. And, above all, I am still standing!

~ So do not fear, for I am with you;
do not be dismayed, for I am your God.
I will strengthen you and help you;
I will uphold you with my righteous right hand.
Isaiah 41:10 (NIV)

Chapter 5

The Fight of My Life:
Realizing the Warrior Within

Patrice Robbins

> "It's not the load that breaks you down, it's the way you carry it."

Question

How do you handle a life or death situation not once but twice?

~5~

Out the wombs of our mothers, the first words spoken into the atmosphere proclaim our entire existence to the world: "It's a girl!" That phrase alone has brought even the brawniest of men to tears. Draped in all pink and frilly dresses, there's just a calming gentleness that accompanies the presence of a little girl. We're simply born that way; innocent, dainty and poised. To be pretty, never to get dirty. To be emotional and nurturing in a world so cold. To play nice and always act like a lady. As women, we are taught to walk away from confrontation with our chin held high and a smile across our face. But when adversity has you cornered and you are forced to fight for your life, what is the rule?

I wish I'd known, as I woke up one morning in excruciating pain. My abdomen ached so badly, I began to pray, doubting I'd be able to make it to the hospital. That "time of the month" didn't cause this kind of twinge. Something was terribly wrong, unusually so.

I immediately called my OBGYN to make an appointment. She suggested I come in for Magnetic Resonance Imaging, or an MRI, just to make sure all was okay. In addition, she brought to my attention that because of my age, it wasn't a bad idea to schedule a baseline mammogram during the same visit. I agreed. The results blew my mind.

The stomach pangs were more than likely caused by an erupted cyst, which I was assured, was nothing to worry about. However, the mammogram exam required a closer look. I was informed that I had dense breast tissue, and more testing was necessary. An ultrasound was recommended. At this point, I was a little more than nervous.

Thankfully, I had a coworker who had gone through this process before. She explained to me what I should expect. "If the doctor comes in after your ultrasound, he or she is going to want to do a biopsy," she warned me. Surely enough, as I waited with sweaty palms at my appointment, in came the doctor.

My heart thumped inside my chest. I'd never before had a biopsy of anything done in my life, yet here I was preparing for my first. I was petrified. The doctor went on to explain her reasoning for concern; my lymph nodes were swollen under both arms. Without further hesitation, my biopsy was scheduled.

Because a sedative was to be utilized during the procedure, I was instructed to have a driver from the hospital. As I was taking all of this in, I was steadily growing more and more afraid. To provide a sense of ease, I was assigned a breast surgical specialist. She was kind and extremely optimistic in the way she spoke. I recall her reviewing the film from my mammogram with such calmness. She told me that everything looked fine and that having eczema could possibly play a part in swollen lymph nodes. This lightened my spirit some. Of course, I'd still have my follow-up appointment, which would reveal the true details of the biopsy.

Worry overtook me all over again as I sat next to my parents waiting to hear the news. The original concern had been with both of my breasts. Thankfully, we learned that my right one was okay. However, my left confirmed what I feared most: cancer.

My entire world changed. Feelings of guilt rushed through me, wondering if I'd somehow been responsible for this calamity. Breast cancer was not in my family history, so why was it happening to me…and at the age of 35? What had I done wrong? What had I not done correctly? The process hit me like a speeding train.

Immediately after receiving a breast cancer diagnosis, I was set up with my team of doctors. My team consisted of my surgeon, radiation oncologist and medical oncologist. Through my journey of appointments, my first visit was with the radiation oncologist. He explained his treatment plan and the side effects of radiation. While the side effects of radiation did not seem too extreme, he did tell me that the medical oncologist would likely advise chemotherapy, which was a bit harsher. The first thing that came to my mind was, *I will be losing my hair.* I had proudly been growing out my natural hair for years and didn't want to lose it, but I did want to take the best course of action to become healthy again.

All of my life my mother had reminded me that I just needed the faith of a mustard seed. A mustard seed was so small and I had that much faith. From that point I said, "I will not need chemotherapy." Faith works! A few days after surgery, my surgeon called to tell me that the tumor was five millimeters and the medical oncologist said that I did not need chemotherapy but I would have to complete 33 rounds of radiation.

I was elated because this was more doable and it gave me hope for a brighter outcome. Sometimes I would tell my friends that it didn't seem like I had cancer because the journey was not as physically intense as I had imagined, but the mental weight of having cancer was very burdensome. The first year or two was extremely difficult because I was always afraid it would come back.

Family and friends were supportive and wanted to see me better. A friend of mine even took me to the grocery store to teach me how to shop more health conscious. At the time, I was not aware of all of the harmful chemicals food manufactures put in our food so they can taste good and have a longer shelf life. These harmful chemicals can contribute to various diseases, such as cancer. Almost instantly, I began eliminating certain things out of my diet. I wanted to be healthy in every way possible. That started with my eating habits.

As the years passed by and my mammograms and MRIs were consistently showing that I was cancer free, the mental struggle of cancer was becoming obsolete. While I'm not saying that I did not get nervous during exam time, I was not thinking as much daily about being a cancer survivor. Slowly, I started slipping into old habits that consisted of eating unhealthy foods and consuming alcoholic beverages, not getting proper rest and allowing myself to stress over matters outside of my control. My drive to maintain a healthy lifestyle faltered.

I began feeling pains, sharp ones. I'd even noticed a little something different while doing my self-exam. I probably should've been quicker to react, but really, what were the chances? What a lesson learned...

It wasn't until I graduated to annual appointments that it happened to me again. Instead of my left breast, this time, it was my right. Shame on me for thinking it couldn't happen twice. But how? I'd done all these genetic tests and didn't carry the breast cancer gene. I was determined to get back on track, and stay on track, with proper nutrition. That was the least I could do for myself.

Meanwhile, I was in a state of panic. My doctor tried her hand again at making sure I stayed positive, but it wasn't as easy the second go-round. The idea of having cancer twice, and only years apart, was weighing on me heavily. For the most part, the same process took place: MRI, ultrasound and biopsy. This time the results seemed especially longer to await, and the doctor who delivered them, unlike my first experience, provided zero comfort. In fact, her words were cold and direct.

"You have cancer again."

Anyone in their right mind would assume as much, but to hear it so blatantly drew this dark cloud over my life. In my mind, there was still hope. This lady was only speculating, but I'd need another biopsy and set of opinions to say for sure. For days, I didn't receive a phone call. No news is good news, right? Wrong.

The following Saturday morning, my phone rang. It was true. According to my pathology report, the odds were against me...again. It was discovered I had Triple Negative breast cancer, the same type I had previously, which predominantly affects African-American (and Hispanic) women such as myself.

The most frustrating factor is that the causes are unknown. No hormones are associated with the cancer, so consequently, there's no personal starting place for a cure. Because Triple Negative is such an aggressive and difficult to treat cancer, my doctors recommended that I do whatever I could to take care of myself. Most importantly, she spoke with me about reducing my stress. Even though I asked why this kept happening to me, my medical team could not say for sure.

Surgery, chemotherapy and radiation are really the only forms of treatment available. I just had to trust and believe that was enough to keep the cancer from reoccurring. It was easier said than done. I prayed this would be the last time I'd ever have to worry about such a terrifying thing.

Contrary to my prior diagnosis, I was informed that I would now have to go through with full treatment, to include chemotherapy. Rightfully so, I decided to consult with a combination of doctors to assure, in fact, that I was being properly instructed. In the process, I met with surgeons, oncologists, and ultimately a naturopathic physician. Ideally, doing anything the natural way appears to be the most attractive option, especially regarding health. But, upon learning this particular doctor only had one successful patient, I was hesitant to go that route.

I was torn between utilizing the natural method, the conventional one, or a combination of both. Whichever way I went would have its own set of pros and cons, so, after much thought, I finally compromised with myself. I'd modify and apply both options. From the natural aspect, plenty of old-fashioned exercise and a better diet, packed with Vitamin C, went in motion. From the scientific side (or the side with actual statistics), I began the dreaded chemotherapy.

To say I was afraid would be putting it mildly. I knew it would get a lot worse before it got better. In spite of everything, I stood firm on faith and my prayers to God. I accepted that this was something I was going to have to go through and the only way I could do it was with Him. I knew He was going to take care of me. No doctor qualified with any fancy degree could tell me differently.

Physically, life became quite painful. But when a few people deemed as close friends started to grow distant, I experienced a different kind of hurt. Chemotherapy slows your lifestyle down tremendously. All the things I once used to do, and still very much would like to have done, I simply did not have the energy to do. By now, my views on life had altered and everything was put into perspective. My eyes opened to the important things. None of that other crazy stuff mattered anymore.

With this awakening came a plethora of sadness. I shed A LOT of tears...and hair. My head was bald, I was losing my eyelashes, my attentiveness wasn't nearly as sharp as it once was, my nails were turning darker—I mean, when I say I cried, I *cried*. Even when I smiled, I was heartbroken inside.

For eight hours, I sat in a chair being injected with one poison, hoping to kill another. My mind wandered, forced to face the reality surrounding me. Family and prayer kept me sane. My parents were there for every treatment. Sometimes I would even FaceTime my brother while I was being treated. Each time I left from chemotherapy physically weakened, yet spiritually strengthened. I held on to the faith the size of a mustard seed, and with that I would make it through this fight.

I am delighted to announce that my treatment journey is complete. I am still working myself back to a place of normality, but I have yet to stop fighting. Funny, I didn't realize how strong I was until unexpectedly catching a glimpse of myself in the mirror. There was no long, flowing hair on my head, nor was there a dainty woman peering back at me. Instead, there stood a fearless, persevering, child of God. For the first time, I recognized the warrior within.

Nowadays, my hair is slowly coming back, as is my energy. I am still unaware what the future holds, but I am no longer afraid. If anything, I am more prepared, equipped with a testimony that can change lives. Having God at the center of my life taught me that despite whatever comes against me, I am already a winner. For the warrior within me is Him, and the battle is never mine to fight.

~ 5 Trust in the LORD with all your heart
and lean not on your own understanding;
6 in all your ways submit to him,
and he will make your paths straight **-Proverbs 3:5-6 (NIV)**

Chapter 6

Bankrupt to Breakthrough:
Birthing the Vision

Davida Bratton

> "You are destined to be more than you are today"

Question

What mindset is God asking you to leave behind, let go of, bankrupt so that He can give you a new revelation?

~6~

When you go from making the most money that you've ever made to barely making ends meet, there is an awakening that accompanies this type of transition. I call it deafening humility. In the fall of 2007, my husband and I thought moving from New Jersey to Virginia to start a new life would be a breeze. Boy, were we in for a surprise.

The original plan had been for us both to attend a local university and obtain post-graduate degrees. By the time we actually moved, we learned that I was pregnant with our first child, so my going to school was placed on the backburner. The new plan was for me to find a job instead, while my husband went forward with obtaining his degree. This was when our previously flourishing financial situation began its first shift to the other side.

That job I *thought* I'd get right away did not happen. Getting adjusted to the move and a new area was expected. Not easily finding employment was an entirely different ball game. Even without the intended graduate degree, I'd been more than qualified. Getting hired on the spot had been the norm for me back in the big city. Why that had suddenly changed was a concept I just could not grasp. My resume spilled over with credible experience and references. Yet, I was still only able to land contractual jobs here and there, and most of those had come from people I knew. Meanwhile, household finances were steadily getting tighter.

Going back to New Jersey, where our income had been higher, crossed my mind on several occasions. I had to ask my husband often, "Are you sure about this?" Oh, how I longed for the financial freedom we'd once had. Still, I didn't give up.

In between my sporadic part-time work, I applied for and landed a job at a nearby university. I was knowingly overqualified, but since the position was fulltime and I was in no place to pass up the consistent extra money, I reluctantly accepted. Boy, did our lives take an unexpected twist! I should have just waited.

The environment, the job itself, the people…it just was not a happy place for most. I'll refrain from giving specifics out of respect for the company, but it was unquestionably unlike anything I'd been accustomed to at previous jobs. The atmosphere provided a whopping daily dose of discomfort. Quitting without a backup plan was something I'd never before done. However, what ultimately took place was the glaring stop sign that my time there had run its course. I had been employed at the university for all of six months before the fat lady sang. To tell you the truth, I wasn't even angry. In fact, I submitted my letter of resignation with poise.

I'd been pregnant with baby number two by then, so I really was okay with alleviating any unnecessary stress around me. On a brighter note, my husband was close to finishing divinity school and was planning to go back into the Air Force as a chaplain. Soon, we'd be leaving Virginia behind for yet another new, but better, life. Ecstatic was an understatement to describe the way I felt. Our situation was becoming so strained that I was relieved to know a change was on its way.

When my husband dropped the bomb on me, I hadn't seen it coming. One month after graduation, he confidently announced, "We're going to start a ministry…here."

Uhm, say what? Just when I was beginning to see light at the end of the tunnel, here he was, taking me for another ride in the dark. Needless to say, I was completely opposed to the idea. The entire time I was thinking that there were plenty of churches around the area that needed great pastors. Why didn't we just start off in one of them? Contrary to my apprehension, we went forth with our ministry anyhow. My emotional bank account was taking a big hit and had not seen any substantial deposits since our arrival in Virginia, four years earlier.

Amidst this journey, we encountered several more hiccups, including our property back in New Jersey. When you have a credit report without a single blemish, you assume nothing can go wrong. Uhm. Well, it did. What was once viewed as an asset quickly became the loathed liability. But I acted like any responsible person would and notified the proper individuals. I discussed establishing a new payment plan; one that would involve the lender taking back the house and letting me go free. Hey…anything is worth a try. What did I have to lose?

I quickly learned my stellar credit score and payment history could not hold a candle to the almighty dollar. I also was told that in order to receive help I had to default my loan. "DEFAULT!" I exclaimed to the lady on the other end of the phone. *Pure craziness!* was my next thought. The only resolution this financial institution could offer this on-time payer with a great credit score was, "Stop paying your bill." Shenanigans!

By this point I was drained and officially bankrupt, with nothing else to give to this life in Virginia. I asked, "What are you doing, God?! What am I not doing? Why is this happening?" Where was this slippery slope taking me? I just wanted off this ride…PLEASE!

A week later, my mother sat in my living room and called me to join her. She was watching a television special on kings and priests by Pastor Bill Winston. During his sermon, he broke down God's system versus the world's system. I found this particularly intriguing. I mean, having formed a personal relationship with Christ as a child, I was well aware there was a difference. All my accomplishments and accolades so far in life, I'd attributed to God. I thanked Him daily for allowing me to be educated and to have these one of a kind experiences. As far as I was concerned, I was operating in the realm God intended for me.

However, hearing this sermon began to open my eyes to what was actually going on in my life. I realized that the world's system and my theology were butting against one another. The worldly standard from my eyes was simply this: If you go to these schools, if you get these jobs, become a productive citizen adding value to the world, then life is going to be great. Well, I'd dotted my I's and crossed my T's and the moment I was in a jam and needed help, they (the world) in return, told me that I had to default on my loan and short sale our house. So, at the end of the day, all the world had to offer me was nothing. Imagine that.

Had I fallen into this emotional and spiritual bankruptcy so that I could be filled with *real* prosperity, the kind of prosperity that reached beyond me? Only time would tell. I began to dig, read and extract the Word, not just speak it like something that was pleasant to contemplate, but would never come to pass. Pie in the sky. And God's system became clearer. Know it, speak it, believe it, walk it, and understand where your rightful place is as a joint heir with Christ. This was the beginning of my mindset shift. All of my thoughts, all of my notions on how I thought things were supposed to happen, I had to redefine. I'd been grasping, almost idolizing in a sense, things that bring us status, financial freedom, and stability with monetary value; my house, my career, my education. It was almost as though if I'd let go of any of these things, it would be the end. But you know what? All of them fell through at some point, and it was not the end. It was in fact the beginning—the beginning of *breakthrough*.

What I did know is that my steps, albeit a little sketchy to me, had already been ordered. Even so, I wondered how many other women, accomplished and successful in their own right, were feeling the same way, like they were coming or had come to the end of their rope; bankrupt – mentally, spiritually, physically and financially. Once "perfection" is but a thing of the past, you're left wondering, *Who am I? Who have I always been? Better yet, what is my purpose?*

I realized that as long as I defined myself by what I've accomplished, I aimlessly strived to compete against myself, a tiresome task at best. Day in and day out, working to be the best, accomplish, achieve and receive accolades. While never spoken, this was what I had been taught was the "way" to achieving the best. However, I was learning that God has called me to live a life built on purpose and not on accomplishments. I was beginning to see a glimmer of light.

While we may be good, even great, at some things, God's only concern is with what He asks of us. So I began to focus more on my spiritual resume rather than the one we print on flimsy paper. Only one of them is everlasting and guaranteed to bring results. And that's the one with the Objective: PURPOSE. After all, nothing tangible comes without an expiration date. You can run out of accomplishments. And no matter how qualified you may be, you can be hired or fired at any time. Circumstances change. Life happens. But purpose is enduring.

The revelation of the call on my life and the charge to co-labor with my husband broke through at my lowest point, when I was bankrupt. And I am so thankful for the process. It's morning for me now. Breakthrough is here, and my God-Vision is in clear sight. Not because life is perfect, but because I've undergone a surgery of sorts, my perspective has shifted and my posture has changed. I don't see life out of the same lenses. The ministry that I was totally against, I have found a new love for. The Life Centre, #tlc757, is thriving and our "Click" campus is in queue to launch this year. I'm excited to announce the *Vida Bratton-Connection Queen* brand, a purpose brand that directs energy toward destiny and advocates for others to do the same. I'm excited to present this year my first initiative, the *Virtuous Womanpreneur* community. The mission of this community is to partner with women, helping them develop their wings, take leaps of faith, and soar in marriage, ministry and marketplace. It is amazing to see what God has done through my *bankruptcy*.

Looking back at all my experiences, particularly my educational background, I never would've guessed I'd be where I am now. But God is making it clear that everything I've gone through and am going through is necessary for where He is taking me. Undergoing the highs and lows of life in order to increase my reach, now that's purpose. It's not about accomplishing any "thing," because God showed me that He alone will provide bountifully and continuously; but to accomplish His purpose for my life. In Him is where all my validation lies. I just have to be ready to walk into the blessing, the blessing that is right around the corner. Daybreak was on the horizon.

In 2011, God gave me a vision of a graveyard full of purpose. Here, people were born and they died without living out the reason they were created. Have you ever tried using lipstick to write? Surely it can serve as an ink pen, but its true intention then loses value, diminishing quickly. The same applies to us. When we are outside of purpose we are being *abused*, drained and depleted with little to no return on our investment.

Credit scores, traffic tickets, grades, jobs, they're all situational and can push out purpose. How one transitions their mind to view what was intended for "change" is where the gold lies. There are people sitting on their purpose because they have bills to pay, children to raise, or some other sort of priority. Their jobs offer longevity and pay generously, so they've inadvertently become convinced that this is as good as it gets. They can't fathom taking a bridge job that would ultimately lead to somewhere better called purpose. It's easy to lose yourself inside the world's way. But discovering God's plan for your life is the most rewarding encounter one could ever endure.

Are you ready to become bankrupt to receive your breakthrough? Let go of your plans, your thoughts, what you must have. Go for broke. Forget what you thought you knew about you. Remove all ideals you think are keys to your best life and really seek God, the Purpose-

Giver. His purposeful preparation will restructure your life in a way that leaves you in constant peace, lacking nothing.

Team Bratton has been living in Virginia just over seven years now. The ministry is growing, lives are being transformed and more of God's purpose and plan is being revealed. Is life a bed of roses? No. The enemy does not like it when a marriage unit is functioning well and making decisions to live a life committed to purpose and transformation. Every day God is pushing me further out into the water and giving me more green lights into the entrepreneurial arena. Most recently I had to leave a job that I totally enjoyed because it was taking up too much of my time. I'm certain this was a test. Would I be willing to move when God instructed, even if it was a "good" job?

The thoughts and strong feelings to retreat are real. Sometimes you may wonder what in the world you have done. But remember, our God is able and faithful. And our actions must match the God-Dreams in our heart. So I no longer depend on the world to dictate my next step in life, my value or worth. I approach culture looking through God's lenses for my life and not looking at God through culture's lenses. And God's Word has remained true in my life. He has never left me nor forsaken me. This is evident daily as He continues to position me in places unimaginable that He equipped me for during "bankruptcy." And the same is true for you. He wants to supply your wants and needs, purposefully. Allow Him to do just that.

~ But seek ye first the kingdom of God, and his righteousness; and all these things shall be added unto you. **Matthew 6:33 (KJV)**

The LemonAid Process

The LemonAid Process only works when you "do it from the Vine," and Christ is that vine, our source of strength. It takes courage, fortitude, perseverance, and #StilettoFaith to embark upon unearthing your LemonAid Process. It will take you on the ride of your life as you are confronted with your "valley" experiences and what you have always known, but often shunned; your Life Purpose Project. It's time to direct your energy toward your destiny. Our prayer is that this process will position you to receive all that God intended for your life. You may want to grab your journal as you embark upon this endeavor. Please pray before starting this activity and allow God to direct your answers. We believe more than you imagined will be revealed. Welcome to your LemonAid Process!

Part I – *The Lemon Squeeze*

You have to understand the lemon and role it plays in your life if you want to ever grasp the fullness of God's purpose for your life. The lemon is a special fruit for a Virtuous Womanpreneur because it embodies the characteristics necessary for success. Let's take a look.

A lemon is:
1. *The leading acid citrus fruit*
2. *Contains Vitamin C, the number one immune boosting vitamin*
3. *Embodies antibacterial agents – great for the throat*
4. *It tightens our pours*
5. *Yellow*, representing the glory of God, His divine nature; holiness; eternal deity; the Godhead. Yellow always speaks of trial and purging.

A lemon is also bitter and is most noted for this characteristic. It has an often overpowering taste that is sharp, pungent, and just not sweet. But it's oh so powerful and life-giving at the same time. The same applies for the lemon(s) in our life, those places that are nasty, burdensome, overpowering, and downright unbearable sometimes. But those same places are life-giving and sweet to so many. If we are to get the goodness out of that lemon, there has to be a *squeezing*. Without the squeezing, the life-changing qualities stay trapped in each bitter pulp.

Question 1: *Which lemons have God given you? What are those "bitter sweet" areas in your life? Where are those places you are feeling led to go that are not glamorous? Is it a ministry, the mission field, entrepreneurship? Use the space below and note at least three.*

A.

B.

C.

D.

E.

A *lemon* doesn't just appear. It is often revealed through life's challenges. And it is often a mirror reflecting our weak places that become our strongest place from which to share. This process has shed new light on 2 *Corinthians 12:9-10 (NIV)*

> 9 But he said to me, "My grace is sufficient for you, for my power is made perfect in weakness." Therefore I will boast all the more gladly about my weaknesses, so that Christ's power may rest on me. 10 That is why, for Christ's sake, I delight in weaknesses, in insults, in hardships, in persecutions, in difficulties. For when I am weak, then I am strong.

At the place we are burdened the most there is strength as noted in each of these six stories. There was a place of revelation where each woman had to deal with herself and recognize, albeit painful, that situation was exactly what was needed to bring forth their purpose. They were being squeezed.

Question 2: *At what point in your journey was each of the lemons you wrote about (above) squeezed and revealed to you? Be specific and note the situation. The very place of your lemon experience will often encompass the DNA of those who are waiting to hear your voice in the marketplace. We can't be afraid to speak about our "bitter" situations.*

F.

G.

H.

I.

J.

Now that you have written some things down, take a moment to reflect on these places where life changed for you; probably in a major way.

Question 3: *What did you learn about yourself during these lemon experiences?*

Iam:

Life is:

I can:

I will:

I want my sister to know:

Lord, I thank you for:

Reflection is good, and so is recognizing those places where lessons were transferred and value added to your life. On your list, there are one or two lemon experiences that stand out and have become the place where your value has become your voice; your voice for others to hear and glean.

Question 4: *Which of the lemons listed has the strongest tug on your heart? While they all may be places where you may put a flag in the ground and become an agent of change, there is one that you know is pungent; pain that has perhaps become your platform to begin walking in purpose. What is that lemon?*

1.

Part II – *The Aids*

There are two pieces to the *Aid* – What God has already told you and what God has already prepared. This is a place of clarity and power. It is that piece that has always been there but goes totally unnoticed. This is partly because we are often in denial regarding the lemon, so we would never discern the Aid(s). When one reaches this phase they are usually more open because they are yielding, somewhat, to the process. With some help from a dear friend, late one night before our first LemonAid Brunch, God downloaded the *Aids* for the lemon-bearer.

What God has told you

1. Where do your **ABILITIES** lie? This may be an area where you are anointed for a particular task. For some this would include areas where you are gifted. Use the lines below to write down at least three abilities. You can write more if you would like.

a.
_____
_____
_____
_____

b.

c.

d.

e.

2. What has God **INSTRUCTED** you to do? Some of you may have an elaborate plan. Others may only have a one word answer. There is no incorrect answer. Reflect and note your answers below. As always, you may have more answers than space provided. Feel free to use your journal.

a.

b.

c.

d.

e.

3. What are your **DOUBTS** and/or **DISAPPOINTMENTS?** You may wonder why this is important. There is a direct connection between this and your lemon. This is usually where the "work" of your purpose is illuminated; where the lemon is exposed. In your valley experience what made you mad, upset, angry, or confused? Write those answers below.

a.

b.

c.

d.

e.

What God has prepared for you

My sister, you are called to birth and build! But God never intended for you to do this alone. Just as the refreshing glass of lemonade cannot be made with lemons alone, neither can your LemonAid be completed. There are ingredients that must be added. Those ingredients are people and resources that have already been positioned, from the beginning of time, to *aid* you. Some will enhance your purpose. Others will make your journey a little sweeter. And still others will be the calm in the whirlwind – a welcomed blessing. I want you to really think out of the box right now. Your perspective has possibly shifted a little throughout this process. Can you identify any of the Aids in your life that are slated to birth and build your purpose? This list may be longer than the others.

a.

b.

c.

d.

e.

f.

g.

h.

i.

j.

_____

_____

_____

_____

_____

Part III – *Stir and Shaking*

Now that everything is in place, the lemon has been squeezed to get juice and pulp, the Aids have been discovered, making the bitter lemon palatable; the stirring and shaking begins. For some this may be uncomfortable, especially if you are a person who never asks for help, are always assisting, and serve as the go-to for everyone else. This is where God begins to show you how much you were not meant to carry; how much excess baggage you've been taking with you unnecessarily. You see, He has only called you to that for which He created you to do. Sometimes we get confused and start doing tons of other things. The beauty, however, is lemons have tough skin, so they can withstand a great deal of friction, setbacks, and hard times. But lemons are also very tender on the inside, a quality necessary to carry out one's purpose with love while appearing unscathed by life's journey. And the most important part of the stirring and shaking is that what's inside begins to mesh together for a greater good. Sometimes seeds appear in the LemonAid. They are taken out and can now be sown into the lives of others. And you are not just sowing anything. You are sowing the revelation from your journey, the experience, the teachings and wisdom; just what your audience needs. There are many who are ready to taste the refreshing LemonAid you have.

Utilizing information you documented above, what is God calling you to sow into the lives of others – Ministry, Marketplace?

_____

_____

_____

_____

_____

What will it do for them? What result will they have?

_____

_____

_____

You are sometimes the AID for others. What do you have to offer in a supportive role to someone else's LemonAid process?

The life you live, my sister, is not your own, but a living sacrifice to be squeezed, stirred and shaken how God pleases to get everything out of you He put inside of you for His Glory. 1 Peter 1:7 tells us:

> 7 *These trials are only to test your faith, to see whether or not it is strong and pure. It is being tested as fire tests gold and purifies it – and your faith is far more precious to God than mere gold; so if your faith remains strong after being tried in the test tube of fiery trials, it will bring you much praise and glory and honor on the day of his return.*

You have now gone through a process similar to what we experienced coming out of our storms, confronted with the reality about our lives, yet knowing *surely* there was more. Each of us began to evaluate and look for reasons why and open ourselves to whatever God wanted. We knew there was more in us, because He allowed us to live through it.

We pray this LemonAid process can aid you in your journey to walking fully in your raison d'etre, the reason for which you were created. You are never alone, sister. You are connected to the Vine just like the lemon. And this is where your strength lies. Please don't forget that. Whether your story is about fear, divine purpose, restoration, faith, trust, breakthrough, or something else, there is a purpose in your pain. It's time to activate your #StilettoFaith and build!

Biographies

Tearanie Parker

Tearanie Parker is a Financial Advisor, Author and Speaker. She graduated from Regent University with a Masters in Education, and also an Endorsement in Leadership. She holds three Securities Licenses and an Insurance license. She is not only licensed in the state of Virginia, but also in North Carolina, Maryland, and Florida. Tearanie Parker's primary focus is personal financial planning, investments, and life insurance. She enjoys educating and helping individuals and their families reach their financial goals. She hosts various workshops that focuses on money management, women and finance, changing the way individuals think about money/and spending habits, and the importance of leaving not just a financial legacy, but a legacy of wisdom, tradition, and values. Tearanie and her husband James have been married for 21 years. They are the parents of four children and they reside in Virginia Beach, VA.

Jacqueline Andrade

Jacqueline Andrade, holds a Bachelor of Arts in Sociology and a Master's degree in Christian Counseling. She has over 20 years experience as a caseworker, and has spent countless hours counseling families, troubled teens and individuals, as well as coaching women and teaching them how to stay married for the long haul. Jacqueline has been happily married for 17 years to her wonderful husband John; they have two boys Jonathan, age 14, and Jarren, age 12. In her spare time she loves to spend time with her family, whether it's supporting the boys with their company Tie Dye Turbros, LLC, cheering for them on the soccer field or watching them play in their school orchestra; pure enjoyment and a blessing is how she describes raising her boys. Jacqueline also enjoys traveling, going to the beach and volunteering. She is involved in her local PTA (Parent Teacher Association) as well as hosting yearly blood drives for the local Red Cross. Jacqueline enjoys teaching at her church and she is also a certified Pilates instructor. It is her lifelong dream to create something for the world that would make life easier for children in the foster care system and those who are affected by trauma and impacted by unexpected loss.

Kimberley Davidson

Born and raised in Houston, Texas, Kimberley Davidson (Kimberley LaTrice) holds a Tourism Master's Degree, a Bachelor's Degree in Business Management, and an Associate's degree in Information Management. She is a former Events Manager with the Department of Defense and has fifteen plus combined years of experience in Event and Protocol arenas. Kimberley is a valued Event

Producer in a myriad of events held in the United States and abroad.

After graduating from high school a year early, Kimberley decided to join the United States Air Force. There she served ten years Active Duty and is currently serving in the United States Air Force Reserves.

After leaving Active Duty, Kimberley combined her passions for food, dining etiquette and fashion into a career in Event Production. She enjoys producing all types of events and puts all she has into making sure those she executes are unforgettable. As a result of her topnotch events, Kimberley has been coined the Martha Stewart of Southern Command (a joint command in Miami, Florida).

Kimberley enjoys doing cross-word puzzle challenges with her three amazingly beautiful children. Together they also enjoy watching the *Food Network Channel* and pretending they are on a cooking show when preparing meals at home.

Kimberley is currently residing in the Virginia Hampton Roads area and is launching the Woman Behind the Hat initiative for women who have been broken and have gone through life situations powerful enough to destroy them, yet have come through the struggles with their faith in God. This movement focuses in the areas of soul ties and restoration. It will produce an annual conference and provide resources needed to help women live and survive a life that God has predestined.

Embracing core values of integrity, innovation and growth, Kimberley continues on a journey of pursuing her purpose to expand the Kingdom of God.

Kimberly Boyd Jenkins

Kimberly Boyd Jenkins is a wife, mother of three, Human Resource manager for her husband's dental practice, as well as a sole proprietor for her own company, AttieMac Resource Group, LLC. Through AttieMac she is an adjunct instructor with The University of Virgin Island's "Weekend Program" teaching students from other countries. In addition, she is an on air radio personality for WHOV 88.1's Gospel Express. Kimberly is a strong advocate for women going through a divorce, as well as dealing with processes thereafter. She hosts events and, of course, does speaking engagements for women's groups, churches, and other organizations. Kimberly is in the process of completing a collaboration with a record label and local artists to host a Gospel Explosion that showcases aspiring artists around the world. In addition, she is working on producing and planning to co-host a talk show to hopefully air on Cable TV.

Residing in Virginia Beach, VA Kimberly holds a B.S. degree in Marketing from Hampton University as well as an A.A.S. degree in Dental Hygiene. Throughout her journey, she realized her purpose in life is to help others streamline and pursue their purpose (or dream) and not become discouraged about the process of getting there, personal shortcomings, or obstacles from past or present.

Patrice Robbins

Patrice Robbins grew up in a rural town in eastern North Carolina and is a graduate of The University of North Carolina at Chapel Hill. After graduating from college, Patrice began to focus her career in the area of Human Resources. Her career has provided opportunities for her to live in New York City and Orlando, Florida. Today she oversees her current organization's EEO & Diversity Program and holds the corporate title of Principal.

In 2009, at the age of 35 during a baseline mammogram, Patrice learned that she had early stage breast cancer. She beat it and, determined to overcome the physical and emotional scarring, she volunteered her time with organizations that provided support to women dealing with breast cancer. Shortly after celebrating her 40th birthday, Patrice learned that she had breast cancer again. While the news was devastating, she relied on her faith in God and supportive family to get her through this journey once again. Patrice is now committed living a healthier lifestyle and sharing her story with others in hopes that it will encourage them. In her spare time, she enjoys preparing healthy meals, traveling and spending time with family and friends.

Davida Bratton

Co-founder of the **Life Purpose Project** and **The Life Centre** with her husband, Ty Bratton, Vida Bratton is committed to encouraging, equipping, and empowering women to accept the invitation to live the life God created them to live, walking in their God-Purpose. She lives out her own God-Purpose co-laboring in ministry with her husband, speaking in the marketplace, and training leaders. Via the Life Purpose Project, LLC, Vida produces experiences that compel women to Develop Wings, Take Leaps of Faith, and Soar! She believes that when energy is directed toward destiny, greatness is the result. Vida is a Consultant, Social Media and Business Strategist, producer of life-giving events, and a Super Connector, affectionately known as the Connection Queen.

This accomplished Womanpreneur has delivered powerful messages to hundreds of people, including entrepreneurs, business owners, and ministry teams. She awakes each day ready to accept her next opportunity to partner with women who are ready to #BeSocial and activate #StilettoFaith. She is excited about her newest endeavor "Virtuous Womanpreneur."

Afterword

These stories were abbreviated snippets of the authors' real life situations. These stories are far from being over and there are more details associated with each story. These authors are already working on separate projects that expound on their chapter written in the *LemonAid Chronicles*.

If you feel a connection to any of these stories, we'd love to hear from you! You can reach out to any of the authors using the information provided below. We want to hear from you - your thoughts, how you would have handled the situation, and any questions you'd like to ask!

Connect with us:

Facebook Group - www.facebook.com/groups/LemonAIDBrunch/
Website: www.eventbrite.com/e/lemonaid-chronicles-book-launch-signing-tickets-16758481068?aff=eac2

Funding An Empire, Tearanie Parker -
Website: www.tearanieparker.com
Twitter: @tearanieparker
Facebook: www.facebook.com/TearanieParker

God, What About Me, Jacqueline Andrade -
Website: www.JacquelineAndrade.com
Twitter: @Jacqueline_Andrade
Facebook: www.facebook.com/AlwaysAPleasureLLC

The Woman Behind the Hat, Kimberley Davidson –
Website: www.KimberleyLatrice.com
Twitter: @WomanBehindHat
Instagram: @Kimberley_LaTrice
LinkedIn: Kimberley LaTrice
Pinterest: Kimberley LaTrice
Facebook: www.facebook.com/KimberleyLaTrice

A Polished Woman, Kimberly Jenkins –
Website:www.IamKimberlyJ.com
Twitter:@Iam_KimberlyJ
Facebook:www.facebook.com/IamKimberlyJ
Instagram: @Iam_KimberlyJ

The Fight of My Life, Patrice Robbins –
Website: www.patricelynette.com
Twitter: @Patrice_Lynette
Instagram: @Patrice_Lynette

Bankrupt to Breakthrough, Vida Bratton –
Website: www.vidabratton.com
Twitter: @VidaBratton
Instagram: @VidaBratton
LinkedIn: Vida Bratton
Pinterest: Vida Bratton
Facebook: www.facebook.com/VidaBratton

LemonAid Journal

LemonAid Chronicles

LemonAid Journal

LemonAid Chronicles

LemonAid Journal

LemonAid Chronicles

LemonAid Journal

LemonAid Chronicles

LemonAid Journal

LemonAid Chronicles

LemonAid Journal

LemonAid Chronicles

LemonAid Journal

LemonAid Chronicles

LemonAid Journal

LemonAid Chronicles

LemonAid Journal

LemonAid Chronicles

LemonAid Journal

LemonAid Chronicles

LemonAid Journal

LemonAid Chronicles

LemonAid Journal

LemonAid Chronicles

LemonAid Journal

LemonAid Chronicles

LemonAid Journal

LemonAid Chronicles

LemonAid Journal

LemonAid Chronicles

LemonAid Journal

LemonAid Chronicles

LemonAid Journal

LemonAid Chronicles

LemonAid Journal

LemonAid Chronicles

LemonAid Journal

LemonAid Chronicles

www.ingramcontent.com/pod-product-compliance
Lightning Source LLC
Chambersburg PA
CBHW060519100426
42743CB00009B/1371